RESILIENCE

INVESTING IN YOURSELF AND YOUR COMMUNITY

ALLEN PRITZLAFF

STORIED
publishing
editing
coaching
storied.pub

ISBN: 978-1-951991-48-7

Typeset by Doug Serven

Cover design by Rohin W. from fiverr.com and Sean Benesh.

Published by Storied Publishing

CONTENTS

INTRODUCTION

The righteous falls seven times and rises again...
Solomon, Proverbs 24:16

Endurance is one of the most difficult disciplines,
but it is to the one who endures that the final victory comes.
Buddha

Our greatest glory is not in never falling,
but in rising every time we fall.
Confucius

Invest in yourself.
Warren Buffett

What is resilience? It is the ability to be flexible, adapt, and survive adverse situations or setbacks. It is a successful response by a person, a family, or a society to changes, disturbances, a tragedy, or a crisis. It is like the Timex watch that "takes a licking and keeps on ticking." It's "true grit"—like what the orphan girl was looking for in the film of that name.[1] It is endurance in the face of a long-term problem or opposition. It's a determination to succeed in spite of the odds against you. It's a powerful impetus that allows a person to move on despite a loss. A super resilient person or group will not only adapt to the loss, but come back even stronger.

But resilience is more than an attitude or an ability to persevere through a crisis. Resilient people take active steps to prepare for possible problems before they happen. Then after a problem appears, they have a tool bag of abilities and assets that can be used to get through or get around the problem. James Bond, Batman, Superman, and nearly all other heroes have an arsenal of abilities and gadgets that get them through difficulties. And if a resilient person faces something beyond their ability to cope with, they are connected with others around them who can help. Conversely, they are prepared to help others to survive an adverse situation.

Life is full of setbacks, whether they affect just you and your family, or your city or region, or the entire country, or the whole world. It doesn't matter who or what caused the setback. You and those around you have to adapt and survive. It is inevitable that challenges and disturbances will come. There are environmental challenges—tornadoes, hurricanes, earthquakes, volcanic eruptions, landslides, floods, snowstorms, droughts, and others. There are widespread economic difficulties—inflation, deflation, recessions, depressions, and financial panics. Individually, many face economic hardships—being laid off; bankruptcy; a serious, expensive illness; a legal setback. There are political changes—new governments and governmental policies, political conflicts, and war. There is crime, both physical and cyber. In many cases, we cannot prevent these calamities, but we

1. *True Grit*, 1969, starring John Wayne. Remake in 2010 with Jeff Bridges

have a choice as to how we prepare for them and how we react to them. This preparation and reaction indicates our resilience.

Examples: An example of resilience is the **British** people in 1940, led by Winston Churchill. They did not give up or give in, even in the face of overwhelming forces arrayed against them. From June of 1940 until June of the next year, they stood against Nazi Germany alone. They were outgunned and outnumbered.

Churchill gave a very stirring speech to the House of Commons on May 13th, 1940, which called for "victory in spite of all terror, victory, however long and hard the road may be. …" He believed in that victory and accepted that it would be a long and hard road to get there. Victory was the goal, and without resilience, success would have been impossible.

A rap-style song popular in Kazakhstan a few years ago has a refrain that begins, "I am **Kazakh**. 1,000 times die, 1,000 times rise up."[2] The rest of the song is about rough times but surviving them in spite of the difficulties. It shows a very resilient spirit, which was needed by the Kazakh people during 70 years of communism. This spirit led them to help one another and use the resources that they had to the best advantage. During the drive to force everyone onto collective farms in the late 1920s, half of the Kazakh population died, but those who survived were able to succeed when conditions improved.

On an individual level, **Dr. Martin Luther King Jr.** was resilient. He endured abuse—oral, written, and physical—and yet he persevered in the goal of racial equality. He kept calm, didn't lose his cool, didn't give up, and kept going.

---

2. Men Qazaqpyn (I am Kazakh), by Yerbolat Kudaybergenov, 2013

Further, he took active steps to prepare himself for every challenge. Today we recognize him as a hero.

Louis Zamperini (1917-2014) was an excellent personal example of resilience. Born in a poor, Italian-speaking family in Los Angeles, he beat the culture of poverty through a sport—middle-distance running. He eventually competed in the 1936 Olympics. He enlisted in the Army Air Forces, was shot down over the Pacific, endured 47 days adrift at sea, and was captured by the Japanese. At a prison camp for several years, he was singled out for particularly rough treatment because of his fame as an Olympic runner and his refusal to make propaganda broadcasts.

After the war, he suffered from what we now call PTSD, but he had a spiritual awakening in 1952, after which he established and ran a camp for at-risk youth, which is still going today. He later returned to Japan in order to forgive the prison commander who had singled him out for terrible treatment. His life was the subject of a book and later a film called *Unbroken* and a sequel. He was the epitome of resilience, but it was more than just an attitude—he trained his body and mind for the Olympics, and this training helped him survive the war. The spiritual foundation he built in the early '50s helped him get through PTSD.

As people groups, almost nothing can match the long-term resilience of the **Israelites** and the **Armenians**, two small peoples who have kept their languages, cultures, and religions intact in the face of overwhelming pressures from larger and more powerful nations around them. The Israelites have existed as a people since Abraham, who lived approximately 2000 BCE, and in particular since the exodus of Abraham's descendants from Egypt and entrance into what is now known as Israel, about 1600 BCE. They were surrounded by larger and much more powerful neighbors—Egyptians, Assyrians, Babylonians, Persians, Greeks, and farther away, the Romans, all of whom conquered and occupied their land at various times.

They have only been independent for short periods of time since 586 BCE, and yet they have kept their distinctive culture, language, alphabet, and religion to this day, even when dispersed as refugees and exiles. They have been resilient in spirit, but also in practical ways. They highly value education and are known for adapting and innovating in every sphere of science and technology.

The Armenians have been a people since the late seventh century BCE. Like the Israelites, they have been surrounded by much larger and more powerful neighbors, and most of their history has consisted of invasions and occupations by those neighbors. Yet they have been resilient and kept their unique culture, language, alphabet, and religion. Like the Israelites, the Armenians prepared for crises through education and spiritual exercises.

In contrast, who today, other than historians, remembers the Hittites, the Goths, and other peoples whose cultures started about the same time as the Israelites and the Armenians? Who can speak the Hittite or Gothic language today? Who knows and keeps alive their culture or religion? Elements of their cultures remain, of course, but not as a whole structure.

Signs of Resilience: Attitudinal signs of personal resilience include calmness, maintaining an even temper, determination, and perseverance in the face of new or acute problems. Outward physical signs include prudence about basic elements of life: power, water, food, and shelter. A society is resilient when its people come together to work on the problem at hand with realistic attitudes without being forced to do so by any authority. Physically, a society is resilient when it thinks ahead about having redundant sources of power, water, food, shelter, and protection from enemies.

In contrast, when an individual is not resilient, problems and unexpected issues will bring on anxiety, distress, anger, despair, or panic. The person is afraid that the problem will be insurmountable and result in a permanent loss of wealth or status. They may be afraid of damage to their health, and the stress reaction to the situation may make their anxiety turn into a self-fulfilling prophecy.

Some fall into abject despair and cannot function. Some lash out and blame the issue on some other person or group. Or a person may mask the problem by abusing alcohol or drugs. Others withdraw from the fray and retreat into a fantasy world of video games. In Japan, there are so many young people, usually men, who retreat from the world in this way that they have a special word for the syndrome—*hikikomori*—literally "pulling inward," but meaning "acute social withdrawal." In short, a person who is not resilient is fragile, and fragile things are always in danger of breaking.

When a society as a whole is not resilient, panic at some level is a nearly certain reaction to the sudden appearance of a problem. One person's panic, rational or not, sometimes leads to mass panic, especially these days when anything can go viral on social media and the 24/7 news cycle. The panic is then multiplied by all of our news and social media reporting on the initial panic.

An example of societal panic would be the American gas crises of 1973 and 1979. A small drop in the supply of oil started panic at the pump, leading to a doubling and then redoubling of the price, odd and even days when you could fill up based on the last digit of your license plate, and long lines. This happened because Americans as individuals, and the nation as a whole, was not prepared and not resilient in the area of transportation. We are only slightly more resilient in this area today. In chapter 7, it will be shown how we as individuals and collectively can be more resilient in transportation.

The long and complex supply chains for our products today multiply the potential problems. One report said that the manufacture of the average pair of blue jeans involves ten different countries.[3] A disaster in any one of them or a transportation problem between any of them could cause business to come to a halt very quickly because of the "just in time" system of production at many companies. This system saves inventory space and cost by having each part involved in a production line arrive there "just in time" to be added to the product.

The system is very efficient, but it is also fragile. Even within North America, a hurricane, flood, or other disaster in one region affects production everywhere else. Part of resilience involves sourcing your most important commodities—water, food, energy and health products—as close to your location as possible. If a disaster happens to your own region, there are ways to bring these items in. But if the well-being of each region is dependent upon the simultaneous well-being of every region, this is not a setup for resilience.

In the late 800s, Norsemen in their very seaworthy longboats discovered Iceland, and having settled the previously uninhabited island, they soon went on to discover **Greenland**, already populated by the Inuit people. The Norsemen created two colonies there, and then went on to discover North America.

But by the year 1420, they had abandoned both Greenland and America. Why? Most people probably think that

---

3. Pike Productions: Globalization is About to Collapse—Here's Why. https://www.youtube.com/watch?v=n7irOJhbwUE

the Norsemen were fishermen because they were famous for their boats, but in fact they were primarily farmers in Norway and everywhere they settled, including Greenland. The period when they discovered Greenland was particularly warm, but then the Little Ice Age descended in the middle of the 1200s and lasted until about 1850. Their crops in Greenland failed, and eventually, they either starved or fled.

But the Inuit people were there when the Norsemen arrived, and they continue to live there to this day. Why did the Norse starve but the Inuit continue to thrive? The Inuit are hunters and fishermen, not farmers. But the Norse would not give up their traditions of farming and learn from the locals. They were physically tough but not resilient in their way of life and, in particular, their preferred food supply.

Independence, Interdependence and "Inter-Independence": Some might think that to be resilient, one must be totally independent and self-sufficient. It could appear that way, but complete self-sufficiency on an individual or family level is not realistic today in most situations. We all rely on specialized medical care, for example, from time to time. Other emergencies can happen that go beyond the ability of an individual, a family, or even a clan or tribe to cope with.

So it is unrealistic to be totally independent, but the current situation of most people in a status of total interdependence can be fragile. This is the case when a family, for example, is interdependent with one particular company or line of work, or a community is a "company town" that is interdependent on the well-being of one particular industry, its supply chain and its customers. Perhaps we need a blend of the two concepts—we strive to be as independent as is practical in our particular environment, but also be connected to a wider network of help when it is necessary.

An example would be the relationships between neighboring fire departments. Each fire department has its own staff and equipment, and in normal situations, they respond to all emergencies within their jurisdiction. They are independent and self-sufficient. But when there is a very large conflagration or other emergency, they invoke mutual aid agreements and help each other.

In recent large fires and earthquakes, emergency teams even come from other countries to help. After the recent large earthquakes in southern Turkey (now called Turkiye), aid not only came from all other parts of Turkiye, but also Europe, North America, and Israel. We might call this "inter-independence." In each of the areas of resilience, we will examine how this might look. For example, how can one increase one's independence and resilience in the provision of electricity, while at the same time helping the wider community become more resilient with their electricity supply.

What Can I Do?: We all have two resources to invest—our time and our money. All of us have the same number of hours in a day, which we spend in some way. If we use those hours in such a way that the next day will be easier or better in some way, then we have invested that time. In the same way, we all have some financial resources, however small. If we just consume the money on something we use that day, then it is gone. But if we take some of the money and use it so that we can continue to benefit from it for weeks, months, or years, then we have successfully invested it. These investments of time and money can be used to make our lives more adaptable to change—more resilient.

This is *not* a self-help book about adjusting your personality to have success and make more money. The concept of resilient investing is how to use your spare time and money to the best advantage, both in normal times and when in unusual adversity.

Resilient self-investing is *not* "prepping" for the collapse of society, although there is some overlap of certain elements. Many "prepping" activities involve stocking up on things that you will use in an emergency or catastrophe. Preparing a certain amount of food, water, and cleaning supplies in case of a natural disaster is a wise idea for everyone. But storing large amounts of these things in your house, garage, or storage shed in preparation for total societal breakdown is another thing altogether.

These stored things do not give you any benefit while they are sitting there, taking up space and becoming outdated. Instead, they soak up your spare money so that those funds cannot be used to invest in something that will pay off in some way now, when there is no emergency, as well as later, when there is one.

Self-investing in the items and knowledge in this book will earn a return for you during normal times, as well as be of great use during an emergency. These are true investments that will benefit you all the time, whether there is a total grid failure—or a zombie apocalypse - or not.

Characteristics of Investments in Resilience:

1. These are activities and financial investments that **benefit you all the time**, whether there is a disaster situation or we are just living in normal times.

2. Investing in yourself and your community will **make both you and your community more self-reliant during an economic downturn**. They are like a second job from which you can't be fired or laid off. Your investment in these things never stops benefiting you, no matter what the situation is in your community, your country, or the world in general. If there is inflation, these investments can shield

some of your costs from going up because you are supplying certain items for yourself.

3. Self-investing **avoids taxes** on the "income" generated because the benefit you receive is generally not in the form of money paid to you by someone else. This may become even more important in the future if taxes are raised. For example, the payback for investing in solar panels is not taxed because it is a reduction (or elimination) of your electric bill, not a payment from someone. If you invest in a sewing machine and make your own clothing, you pay no sales tax on those clothes, nor do you pay income tax on money you would have had to earn to buy clothes the usual way.

4. Each area of investment **can start very small and be done step by step**, just like putting money in a savings account. You can start with an investment of $10, or just a few minutes a day. As you obtain more money and/or time, you can go up from level to level in each of the 12 areas of investment. Ultimately, you could reach the point of total independence for an area of life, such as energy, food, or water. Most people will not even aspire to that ultimate level because it may not be practical in their situation. But you can go partway there in several areas, and every step you go in that direction makes you and the people around you more resilient.

5. These investments in yourself are **not subject to outside forces** such as discrimination, racism, sexism, or, in most cases, government control. You control how much and when you want to invest and when it is enough for you in each area of investing.

There are 12 basic areas of life that will be covered in this book in 12 chapters. For each area, there will be levels that a person can work on. Level 1 will give easy, simple, and cheap steps that a person can do to increase resilience in that area of life. Level 2 will take these steps further, and so on. The 12 basic areas are:

- electricity,
- cooking and hot water,
- heating and cooling your house,
- sources of food,
- cooking and preserving food,
- water,
- transportation,
- skills for living,
- finances,
- health,
- emotional and spiritual,
- and networking.

CHAPTER 1
ELECTRICAL ENERGY

If you were to remove everything from our lives that depends on electricity to function, homes and offices would become no more than the chambers and passages of limestone caves —simple shelter from wind and rain, far less useful than the first homes at Plymouth Plantation or a wigwam.

Jane Brox

Electricity Powers Modern Life: Electricity is essential for modern life, and in the United States, we use a lot of it. The average household uses almost 900 kilowatt hours (kWh) per month.[1] At an average cost of 13 cents per kWh in 2020, this means a monthly bill of about $115.[2] However, that is only part of the story. Industry, businesses, and government also use a lot of electricity. All together, America generates about 4.3 trillion kWh per year including privately generated solar

1. https://www.eia.gov
2. https://www.electricate.com

power, or an average of 18,700 kWh per person. If we assume a household size of 2.5 people, then this means 46,723 kWh per household per year, or 3,894 kWh per month, which costs an average of $506 per month.[3]

It Can Be Gone Tomorrow: What would you do if the electric grid went down for a day? How about three days? A week? How would you keep food cold, if it were summer? How would you keep warm, it it were winter? What would you do if your car broke down in the middle of nowhere and your phone was on 1%?

When our energy supply is damaged, as in a hurricane, tornado, earthquake, or other disaster, it affects not only the homes and businesses that are damaged directly, but everyone in the city or region, sometimes for many days, as happened in Texas in February 2021 during a severe ice storm, or during Hurricane Ian in Florida in September 2022. If you are prepared to be resilient, then your food will not spoil, your phone will continue to be charged, you will have alternate sources of water and heat, and you will be in a position to help others who are in a bad way due to the disaster.

On top of these more common natural disasters, a large coronal mass ejection (CME) could hit the earth at any time. This is when a magnetic storm on the sun ejects millions of tons of material. If this material goes in the direction of Earth, it could take down the electrical grid over all of North America for months if not longer.

This is because the thousands of miles of electric lines would act as an antenna, collect the energy of these solar particles, and could overload and blow out many transformers, many of which are custom made for each location,

3. https://www.statista.com

without backups. A CME happened in 1989 in northeastern North America which blacked out all of Quebec for nine hours and damaged transformers as far away as New Jersey.[4]

A similar large-scale failure of the electric grid could be caused by a cyber attack, an electro-magnetic pulse (EMP) caused by the high altitude detonation of a nuclear bomb, or a physical attack on less than a dozen key connection points of the North American power grid. Our power grids are only partially protected against any of these possible events. The more you are personally prepared, the more resilient you will be. And you can be personally prepared because electricity is one of the few forms of energy that a private person can generate for themselves.

HELP YOURSELF

- An investment in a resilient personal electrical supply pays "interest" or a "dividend" in the form of a reduction or elimination of what you would otherwise pay someone else for this same energy.
- This dividend is not taxed, as most other dividends or interest would be. This adds 10% or more to the value of this investment, compared to other investments.
- If your children go to college, you must fill out the FAFSA form for potential financial aid. This form asks for income from your federal income tax form 1040, and also asks for all of your financial assets, not including your house or your retirement funds. Money that you have invested in energy conservation or production would not

4. https://www.livescience.com/carrington-event

be counted, whereas the amounts you put in any common financial investment, such as bank accounts, stocks, and bonds, are counted against you.

HELP YOUR COMMUNITY

- You reduce the use of nonrenewable resources (fossil fuels) used to produce electricity that will someday run out, thus making the whole human race more resilient.
- You reduce the reliance of your community on oil and other fossil fuels from unstable parts of the world, thus making your country as a whole more resilient.
- You reduce the emission of harmful air pollution.
- Most of these sources will reduce the emissions of carbon dioxide, which contributes to global climate change.
- The more that you are self-sufficient or independent in this area, the more you can help your neighbors in the case of an emergency. This is being inter-independent.

Step by Step: As in all of the 12 areas of resilience, electrical energy is a part of our lives that we can **begin with baby steps** and progress as we have the ability. Ultimately, if a person uses all the appropriate means available to us now, it is possible to achieve "net zero" energy use no matter where you live—even in extremely hot or cold climates. This means that over the space of a year, a house will produce as much energy as it consumes. It is averaged because most electrical energy produced by individuals come from solar panels, which generate less energy in the winter, when more energy is needed.

Even in Canada and in northern states of the U.S., with cold winters during which there are fewer hours of sunlight, houses have been built that use no net energy from outside sources over a year period.[5] This has been done by working on three areas: conserving energy through insulation and modern appliances, making use of passive energy as much as possible, and the use of solar panels and/or wind turbines.

It is also possible today to build "off grid" houses in any climate zone, which do not use any outside energy at any time. This is more difficult because more energy storage is necessary for those times of the year when production is insufficient. But today, energy storage is commercially available for individual homeowners.

Our personal uses of electrical energy are many. We use it for lighting, heating and cooling our homes, for cooking, for making hot water, for powering some of our transportation, and for powering or charging all of our entertainment and communication devices—televisions, Wi-Fi, computers, tablets, and cellphones. These many uses mean that we must consider how to supply them in order to be resilient.

Producing Your Own Electricity: The most common ways that most people can produce their own electricity are solar electric panels (also known as photovoltaic, or **PV panels**), **wind turbines**, and small-scale **hydroelectric turbines**. PV panels come in all sizes, from tiny ones on calculators to

---

5. A net zero house has been built in Calgary, Alberta, where it is -40 degrees in the winter. See https://www.youtube.com/watch?v=KbJLSrx-jXI

ones designed to mount on a building. Today, wind and hydroelectric turbines are also available in sizes appropriate for a homeowner.

The disadvantage of solar panels compared to the other two sources today is that 60% of the various materials and steps to create an American-assembled solar panel are done in China, and this rises to 70% of the panels assembled in other South-East Asian countries.[6] Supply chain disruptions can thus derail the deployment of a system. Many small, homeowner-oriented wind turbines are also made in China, but the technology is not complex, and a simple turbine could be assembled by a hobbyist using common parts available anywhere. Small hydroelectric systems can be made the same way. In contrast, growing and cutting wafers of silicon crystals for solar panels cannot be done by hobbyists.

Wind turbines come in different sizes but must be fixed to one location. They are only warranted if you live in an area with fairly strong, steady winds. Usually, this means rural and not urban areas because urban areas have many objects that obstruct the wind—buildings and trees. Even the ground itself slows down the wind, so higher and more consistent wind speeds are found higher up. Unless you live on a high-rise penthouse, your wind turbine in an urban area will not be more than 10 meters off the ground. Consistent winds are usually found more than 50 meters off the ground. The power of wind varies according to the cube of the wind speed. Therefore, an increase of wind from 5 mph to 6 mph, only a 20% increase in speed, increases the power by 73%.

If you live where it is windy only part of the time, a wind turbine is usually not worth the cost compared with solar panels. Wind turbines start producing energy at wind speeds

---

6. https://www.statista.com/chart/24687/solar-panel-global-market-shares-by-production-steps/

of 5 to 8 mph, but their rated performance (told in ads and printed on the box) is measured at much higher wind speeds, such as 15 mph. Therefore, the relative merits of wind and solar power depend on where you are located. If you are in a windy area that is cloudy and rainy most of the time, or perhaps at a high latitude where there is very little sunlight during the winter, then wind power might be your way to go, or perhaps a combination of wind and solar. You must also consider that wind turbines involve moving parts, which eventually wear out. In contrast, solar panels do not involve moving parts, although they do degrade slowly over long periods of time (decades).

Hydroelectric generation is possible for hikers with a tiny portable system, and there are many sizes for people living in rural areas who have a stream or small river on their property. Modest amounts of electricity can also be obtained through **thermo-electric generators**. **Human-powered electrical generation** is also possible on a very small scale.

Electricity production is a perfect example of how you can start small and work your way up. Here are five levels of resilience:

LEVEL 1: SMALL-DEVICE CHARGING, AND ENERGY CONSERVATION

Solar Small-Device Charging: You can start small in solar energy with just a solar flashlight and a solar small-device charger, and work up from there. A solar powered flashlight can be bought for as little as $10. It will save you money because you will never have to buy

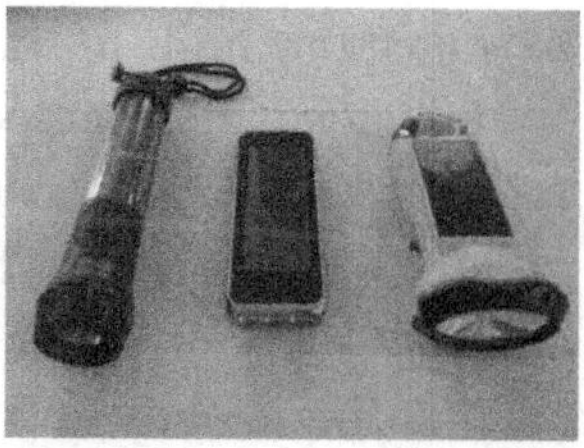

Three examples of solar flashlights. (My photo)

batteries for it. There is nothing more frustrating than grabbing a flashlight when you need it and finding out that the batteries are dead (or worse—dead and leaking, thus damaging the contacts). If you leave a solar flashlight in a place that gets at least some light, it will always be ready. Some solar flashlights have a secondary power source such as a hand crank generator.

A small solar power bank, foreground, in comparison to a smartphone. (My photo) It will charge a cell phone at least one time but will take several days to recharge in the sun.

Small-device chargers with a built-in solar panel, also known as solar power banks, start at about $20 and are about the size and shape of a thick smartphone. They can charge your cellphone, tablet or other small devices. These can be used day-to-day, are very handy when traveling or backpacking, and would be crucial in a blackout situation. Most of these small device chargers also include a flashlight. Any solar powered devices like these should be stored in an open area where they can be charged by sunlight every day. If they are put in a drawer or stored anywhere dark, they will slowly lose their charge. After some years in that condition, they will be dead and will not take a charge anymore. Most small solar power banks have just one built-in solar panel.

Other small solar power banks have four or even five fold-out panels that can charge up the bank much more rapidly when needed. These start at about $35. One of these has kept my cell phone charged for several winter months, even during cloudy and rainy days. Both the solar flashlight and small-device chargers are very useful for camping and backpacking, especially trips that last for a number of days.

Small multi-function solar power banks are also available.

The one at the right has an LED flashlight and a radio with emergency weather and short-wave bands. It has a USB outlet for charging other small devices, and a hand crank for emergencies when there is no sunlight. It is next to a smartphone for size comparison.

Small, portable **hydroelectric chargers** are also available. This is an apparatus that has a small propeller in it that spins a small generator. You anchor the generator to the bank or other fixed location with a line and let it spin in the current of a stream. The anchoring line includes a wire conducting the electricity it generates to a small container with a battery, from which you can keep a few small devices charged up. One version of this type, the Waterlily, costs about $200 and claims an output of 360 watt-hours per day, roughly comparable to a 100-watt solar panel.[7] The advantage is that it can be used for remote camping in the event that a lot of sunshine is not available for a solar unit, such as in a thick forest. Since the unit weighs nearly 3 pounds, a small solar power bank at $10 to $35 would be a lighter and cheaper choice for backpacking under most conditions.

Human-Powered Energy: It is possible to generate small amounts of power by cranking a small generator by hand. Some small flashlights and radios made for emergencies have hand cranks.

7. https://shop.waterlilyturbine.com/

On a slightly higher level, there are foot pedal-powered generators. One firm, K-Tor, sells a compact one that sits on the floor while you sit on your own chair.[8] It can produce up to 3 amps at 14 volts (42 watts), for charging a 12 volt battery. You could sit at such a machine and read a book while charging your battery, and at the same time get some exercise (see Chapter 10: Health).

Energy Conservation: Starting small, you can also invest in energy conservation. A first step is to make sure that all the light bulbs in your house are LED. They are about six times more efficient than the old incandescent bulbs. They are also twice as efficient as the compact florescent (CFL) bulbs that replaced the incandescent bulbs. LEDs last 20 times as long as incandescent bulbs, and three times longer than CFLs, therefore justifying their higher price. Also, unlike CFLs, they can be used with a dimmer for mood lighting. As an added bonus, since LEDs use much less power, they will not heat up your house on hot summer nights. Also, LEDs do not contain any harmful elements or chemicals, like CFLs. See the chart below:

60 W incandescent

(800 lumens)
last 3,000 hours
$1 each (decorative bulbs only)
Cost/100 hours: $0.84

16-24 W CFL

(800 lumens)
last 8,000 hours

8. https://k-tor.com

no longer available
Cost/100 hours: $0.28

8-12 W LED
(800 lumens)
lasts 10,000 hours
$2 each
Cost/100 hours: $0.14 plus cost to buy

You can also save energy by drying your clothes the old-fashioned way, on a clothesline, at least when the weather is nice.

Savings from this step that can be invested: 1. No need to buy flashlight batteries. 2. Decreases in electric bill due to fewer watts used for lights, and less heat produced by lighting in summer.

LEVEL 2: PORTABLE POWER BANK SYSTEM WITH SOLAR PANELS AND/OR SMALL WIND TURBINE, THERMO-ELECTRIC GENERATOR

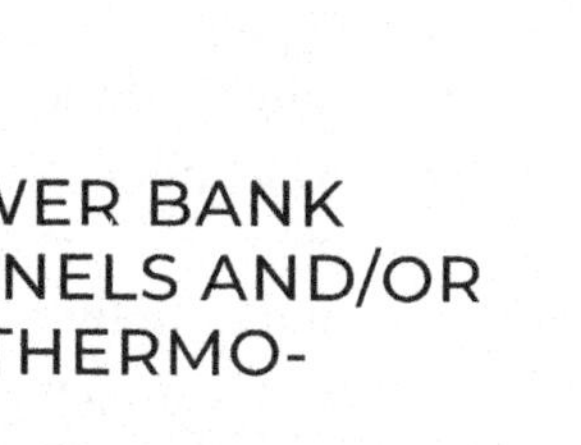

Small Power Bank: This involves a small stand-alone power bank (also called a "portable power station") and one or more small solar panels or other generating source. They are often misnamed "solar generators" even though they can be charged up from sources other than solar, and by themselves, they do not generate any power—they only store it.

A small power bank is about the size of a short, fat loaf of bread, and they have become popular, so there are many companies making them and competition has lowered the prices. These can charge up several devices like cellphones at one time, since they have several USB connectors. They have a 12 V "cigarette lighter" style outlet, and also one or more 110 volt outlets that can power things such as computers, Wi-Fi and routers, televisions, CPAP machines, and other small medical devices. The smallest, rated at 200 watt-hours, (pictured—photo from http://www.goalzero.com) start at about $200, and some include a small solar panel rated at 60-100 watts.

In ordinary times, you could power your laptop computer, Wi-Fi, cellphones, and a few LED lights with such a unit, thus achieving some savings on your electric bill. Also, if the power were to go out, your computer and your connectivity would be unaffected. They are also very useful for car camping—they can provide light for your campsite without using batteries, candles, or propane lanterns, and will keep your phones charged. Small LED lights are available that plug into the USB sockets on these power banks. When obtaining lights to be used with power banks, consider that converting the power from 12 volts DC to 110 volts AC involves some loss. Therefore, it would be more efficient to use lights that run from either the 12 volt or USB outlets.

Parts of a Power Bank: Any power bank and charging system actually consists of four parts: a **generation method**, a **charge controller**, one or more **batteries**, and an **inverter**. All solar panels, small hydroelectric generators, and wind generators generate direct current (DC). If the voltage supplied by the source is above that of the battery, the battery will be charged by the source. But between the two is a charge controller. When the battery is fully charged, the controller will shut off any further charging to avoid damage to the battery from overcharging.

The fourth part is an inverter. This converts the DC of the battery, which is 12 volts in smaller systems, into the 110 volt alternating current (AC) used by most appliances in North America. The number in the designation of these units usually indicates the maximum number of watts that the inverter can deliver continuously, such as 200 or 250 in the smallest ones. For some units, there is also a higher number that indicates "peak" or "surge" performance. This means that the unit can deliver a higher number of watts for a short time, usually about a minute or two. Most loads that include a motor, such as compressor type refrigerators or fans, require a higher number of watts for the motor or compressor to start functioning, but once they are going, they need a lower number.

We had a small stand-alone solar system for a while, with a 500 watt inverter without any surge capacity. This was theoretically enough to power our refrigerator, but the compressor needed a higher wattage for a few seconds to start up. Thus, when we plugged the refrigerator into it, the inverter immediately made a loud chirp as the safety circuit shut off the device. We needed a larger inverter, or one with a surge capacity. To be safe, double the wattage rating of any motor to determine the peak wattage needed to be supplied by your inverter.

Small wind turbines are another way to produce power. Numerous models of small wind turbines have been available for many years because boat owners use them to provide a small amount of power to their boats that are anchored out in a bay with no access to shore power. More recently, they are also becoming more popular among homeowners. They have a diameter of about 3 or 4 feet, and weigh between 13 and 17 pounds. They are usually rated to produce 400 watts, but this rating is with a wind speed of 29 mph, which the average person is not likely to encounter very often. More realistically, such a unit will generate about 100 watts if the wind is blowing at 13 mph, and in those conditions over 24 hours they will produce about 2.4 kWh. They start at about $200, but can cost up to $800, so you must do some homework to find the balance between cost and quality. They can easily be mounted on the roof of your house, or any high place free of surrounding obstructions. Small wind turbines like these are typically made to charge a 12 volt battery.

Until recently, all wind generators have involved blades, either spinning around a horizontal axis (the most common, known as HAWT—Horizontal Axis Wind Turbine) or around a vertical axis (VAWT). HAWTs are slightly more efficient, but their disadvantage is that the generator must be at the top of the pole, which is inconvenient for any maintenance.

VAWTs are of two types—Savonius (named after Sigurd Savonius, a Finnish engineer, who invented this type in 1922) and Darrieus (named after Georges Darrieus, a French engineer, who invented this type in 1926). Savonius turbines resemble cups turned sideways spinning around the vertical axis, and are also called "drag-type." Darrieus turbines consist of two or more curved aerofoil blades and resemble an eggbeater. The advantage of VAWTs is that they can easily cope with wind coming from various directions, which often happens around obstructions such as hills, buildings or trees. Both HAWTs and VAWTs are made in small sizes for homes or boats.

Bladeless wind generators are now being developed. One

design consists of a tower, the major portion of which can oscillate slightly side to side due to the turbulence of the wind flowing around it on both sides, thus producing power. According to experiments, a tower 1 meter tall could produce 3 watts, and a 2.75-meter-tall tower could produce 100 watts, about the power of a small solar panel during daylight.[9] For Level 4, a tower of 9 meters could produce 1 kilowatt. The power output of these towers increases as the square of the height. They are omni-directional and could be placed near buildings, trees, or other obstructions, unlike HAWT generators. They are also safe for birds, unlike turbines. However, for the same ground footprint, they produce less power.

Another bladeless wind generator on the development horizon uses electrostatic principles. Unlike the towers mentioned above, these have absolutely no moving parts. A working prototype has been tested in the Netherlands.[10] It has a series of wires in one open box-like structure, with one set being positively charged and the other negative, separated by a few inches of air. Look for this technology, as well as the towers, to become viable and commercially available in the future.

About 45 Watts of power can be obtained with a **thermoelectric generator** placed on top of a heat source such as a wood stove.[11] This could be a good choice for an off-grid cabin in a forest with limited opportunities for solar panels or wind turbines.

Savings from this step that can be invested: Decrease in electric bill due to some devices and lamps plugged into

---

9. https://www.youtube.com/watch?v=pS2mhjdKdAA
10. https://www.youtube.com/watch?v=nNp21zTeCDc
11. https://www.tegmart.com/thermoelectric-generators/wood-stove-air-cooled-45w-teg

solar power, particularly during peak hours in the late afternoon.

LEVEL 3: LARGE PORTABLE POWER BANK AND CHARGING SYSTEM

A larger stand-alone solar, wind, or hydroelectric system rated at 1000 watts or higher would power your standard home refrigerator plus a number of smaller devices. A standard-size home refrigerator uses about 450 kilowatt hours per year or 1.23 kilowatt hours per day. A solar panel usually produces about five times its rated power per day. Thus a 100-watt panel will produce about 500 watt hours (half of a kilowatt hour) in a day, figuring an average equivalent of five hours of direct sun per day, summer and winter.

The sun is out more hours than that, but unless you have a system that continuously angles the panels to face the sun, the sun will be hitting the panels at a slant most of the time, thus producing fewer watts. Therefore, to run a refrigerator with a power bank alone would require at least 400 watts of solar panels, allowing for losses due to converting the DC from the panels to AC for your refrigerator. This power bank could also be connected to a wind turbine.

If you used such a system day by day, then your electric bill would only be for electric cooking devices, such as a stove or microwave oven, which use more power than a refrigerator. With such a system, if there were to be a power outage of several days, your food would not spoil, and you could still be connected to Wi-Fi, your cellphone would not lose power, and you would still have some lighting.

This power bank would be the size of a small microwave oven and cost from $750 and up, and the 400 watts of solar panels would cost about $320. Shown above is a 3000-watt maximum power output system with two 2000-watt-hour batteries (total 4 kWh).[12] A 900-watt room air conditioner is plugged into it. It is charged by 950 watts of solar panels located on the patio of a condo. It also powers several computers and lights in normal conditions, but would also power the owner's refrigerator and Instant Pot if the power were to go out.

Even if you do not have solar cells for your power bank, it will benefit both you and your community in two ways because many communities are now going to "time of use" metering. For example, in my community, the highest usage for electricity is from 4 to 9 pm, so they charge more for electricity during those hours. Therefore, you can use the energy in your power bank during those hours, and charge it up again during the off-peak hours. This saves you money on your electric bill and helps the community smooth out the need for power.

Savings from this step that can be invested: Increased savings on electric bill due to shifting usage from peak hours to non-peak, if on a time-of-use plan.

LEVEL 4: FIXED SOLAR PANEL ARRAY, WIND TURBINE OR HYDROELECTRIC SYSTEM, GRID-TIED

Solar Panel Array: At this level, you invest in six to 20 solar panels which are installed on the roof of your house or

12. Author's photo of his son-in-law's system.

garage, or on a rack on the ground near your house, and/or a wind turbine. The wind turbine could also be on your roof or on top of a pole.

My own 11 panels

Depending on your state laws and your utility provider, you would pay $5 to $10 per month for the privilege of connecting to the grid. At the end of the year, you would pay for any power you used over and above what your panels or turbine produced. If you produced an excess of power, the utility might pay you for it, but probably at the wholesale rate, which would be rather low. Thus, you should carefully calculate how much electricity you use during a normal year and install the number of panels and wind turbines so as to produce that amount and no more under normal circumstances. If you wish to install a solar system but do not have enough money to buy a large enough system to cover your entire electric bill, then just buy enough to ensure that you are no longer in the top tier of cost per kilowatt hour.

Agro PV: On a larger scale, if you are a farmer or have a large garden, PV panels can be spaced out above your growing crops. It is sometimes called "agri-voltaics." This helps in three ways. First of all, most crops do not use 100% of incoming solar radiation if they are in full sun. Any radiation above what they can use just causes them to "sweat," thus wasting water resources. In addition, solar panels perform more efficiently when they are not hot, and placing them above growing crops cools them. Therefore, solar panels placed 10 to 15 feet above crops results in more energy production, less water use, and more comfortable farmers who can work in partial shade! See several websites in Appendix 2 for more information under the heading "AgroPhotoVoltaics."

In addition, a study at the University of Arizona found that shade-tolerant crops such as lettuce, peppers and tomatoes grown under PV panels had increases in yields of up to 300%.[13] They did very well in the partially shady, cooler, and slightly more humid conditions under the panels.

Larger wind turbines could be mounted on a house in a strong location, or on a tall pole that has been stabilized with guy wires. These are not the gargantuan machines seen in commercial wind farms, but have blades about 4 to 5 feet in diameter, and weigh about 40-60 pounds. These can produce about 12 kWh per day (if there is wind all day), and cost about $2,000 not including installation. They are made to charge 12, 24, or 48-volt battery banks.

Wind turbines for home use can be with a horizontal or a vertical axis. Horizontal axis wind turbines (HAWT) spin like a fan, with the shaft in a horizontal position, whereas vertical axis wind turbines (VAWT) spin like a top, with the shaft aligned vertically. HAWTs are slightly more efficient but more complex. The blades of a HAWT are shaped like wings, and must be precisely shaped because their tips are moving much more rapidly than the area near the center. The HAWT must have a vane or other mechanism to keep the blades facing into the wind.

In contrast, a VAWT can spin with wind coming from any direction and is therefore more efficient at catching the gusty and changeable winds prevalent in urban environments or other places where there are obstructions. The blades are

---

13. Undecided with Matt Ferrell: How Solar Panels are Changing Agriculture—Agrivoltaics Revisited, https://www.youtube.com/watch?v=ww-_U7_oQbY

simpler to design and make because all parts of the blades are spinning at the same speed. Also, with a VAWT the actual generator mechanism is at the bottom of the fan blade assembly, whereas with the HAWT, the generator is at the hub, which is usually high off the ground, therefore complicating any maintenance or repair.

Small Hydroelectric Generators: A permanently installed small hydroelectric generator can also be a part of such a system. You create a small dam on a stream on your property and pipe some water downhill to a turbine. In many places a dam is not necessary—you simply divert some of the stream into a pipe and, after the turbine, send the same water back to the stream. This is called a "run-of-river" system and creates fewer potential ecological disruptions. Some people have made generators out of a washing machine or other similarly sized motors, but ready-made systems are now being produced. They start at about $12 for a very small unit with ½ inch pipe threads on both sides. This produces about 10 watts, or 240 watt-hours per day, which is enough for a few small electrical devices.[14] Units scale up from there.

The amount of energy they can generate depends on the volume of water in your stream and how much "head" you have, that is, the vertical distance that the water drops in your pipe from the source to the turbine. They are usually made to charge a 12-volt battery. If you have a good-sized stream, you may be able to power your entire house. The average house uses 900 kWh per month, or 30 kWh per day, which would need a unit producing 1.25 kilowatts (1250 watts). A turbine of this size would cost about $1,000 not

14. https://www.amazon.com/wonofa-Generator-Turbine-hydroelectric-Portable/dp/B07JY62J3B

including the installation of a small dam and the pipes (penstock) that would be required. A more energy-efficient house might be able to be powered by a 500-watt turbine, costing only $250.

If you live in a forested area where solar panels would be shaded and the wind would be obstructed, but you have a stream, this would be a good option. The good part about hydroelectric power is that it generally produces the same amount of energy 24 hours per day, every day, unlike solar and wind power. However, some people have constructed small hydro systems even on seasonal streams, for use during the winter when solar power is at a minimum.

If your property contains a slow-moving but deeper stream of water, a firm in Ontario, Canada, is developing a "waterotor" that can produce electricity.[15] A 1-kilowatt generator requires 44 inches of water moving 2-4 mph and costs about $5,000. They have larger units that will produce 10 kilowatts or 1 megawatt.

Upgrading—Have You Wasted Money? If you have previously been at Level 3 and already have a large portable power bank and some solar panels, has this investment been wasted if you then install solar panels to power your whole house? Not at all. You can continue to power certain things from your Level 3 system, which means that you do not need to buy as many solar panels for your house. You then have two systems, which gives you maximum resilience in case of a prolonged power outage.

If you have an electric or plug-in hybrid car, your transportation fuel is covered by this Level 4 investment. If you have an electric stove, then your cooking fuel is also

15. http://www.wateroter.com

covered. It could also be possible to heat your house with electricity from solar panels if your climate is not too cold.

Cost—Cheaper Every Year: This level would require an investment of about $9,000 and up. The cost of solar panels has been dropping on a per-watt basis—they were 12 times cheaper in 2020 than they were in 2010. The panels themselves are also more powerful. My own 11 panels on my current house produce more energy than the 16 panels of the same size on our previous house, which were installed in 2006, and the 11 panels were cheaper to purchase. Panels in 2006 typically were rated at about 200 watts, but the same-sized panels in 2023 produce about 360 watts.

You should be aware that if the electric grid goes down for any reason, your power will also go off, even though you have solar panels. This is because there would be utility people repairing the lines, and if your panels were still connected to the grid, the workers could be electrocuted.

Also, you cannot just plug your refrigerator or any other electrical load directly into the large inverter that goes with your panels because there must be a match between the energy supplied and the load connected to it. This is why they do not give you an electrical outlet on your inverter. A battery and its associated charge controller supplies that match, which would be the next level.

Since the solar panels or wind turbines are in a fixed location, this location is very important. Optimally, the solar panels would be facing south at an angle to maximize solar radiation to the panels at noon in December, with no trees or other buildings blocking the sun. The next best is to have the panels facing southwest or west, so as to produce more energy in the afternoon and early evening. For wind turbines, the higher the better, and they should be clear of any obstructions such as trees and other buildings.

Example of a grid-tied system: We installed a grid-tied solar panel system in 2006. When there were five people in our household, our electric production was slightly less than our usage, so our "true-up" payment for a year of electricity was usually about $50. Later, we became empty nesters, and our usage went down, so that the last year we lived there, we paid less than $5 at the end of the year. This included an electric stove and an electric clothes dryer. Thus, our investment in a solar system paid a "dividend" immediately, and this dividend was not taxed.

Savings from this step that can be invested: It may seem like the payback for a system like this is rather small. However, consider that the interest rates today at a bank are about 4% at best, and other investments can be risky. The payback for solar panels is virtually guaranteed because there will always be a customer for the electricity they produce—you and your family. On top of this, when you sell your home, the solar panels add to the value of your home, and you will get your investment back!

In addition to zeroing your electric bill, if your system is large enough, you can also reduce your bills for natural gas. This winter we used electric space heaters powered by our solar panels instead of our gas furnace. Bills for natural gas in our area tripled, whereas ours stayed low—only $25 for the month of January. The previous January we paid $75, so our bill would have been about $225 had we continued to use gas.

Part of our monthly budget for gasoline is also saved since we have a plug-in hybrid. About 200 miles per month in local driving is covered, thus saving at least $30.

LEVEL 5: GRID-TIED SYSTEM WITH BATTERY BACKUP

This is a Level 4 grid-tied system with the addition of a large power bank, so that you are prepared for emergencies. Tesla, Enphase, LG, and other companies are producing these systems. The system is configured so that it automatically disconnects from the grid when it goes off, and your solar panels then charge your power bank through its charge controller. This system certainly would handle most tasks, including lights, coffee makers, microwave ovens, refrigerators and freezers, fans, small portable electric heaters, and room air conditioners. If you have a very large system, it may also handle a 220 volt stove, clothes dryer, a whole-house air conditioning and heating system, or charge your electric car.

Such systems can be useful from day-to-day, and not just for emergencies. They can be set up so that your house does not draw any energy from the grid during peak hours, when energy costs are high, say from 4:00 to 9:00 p.m. as in my area. During the off-peak hours when energy costs are lower, your system would automatically charge the battery again. This would save you money, and also help the community smooth out electric demand.

The Tesla Powerwall and other similar power systems use lithium batteries. But a new system of energy storage using hydrogen is just now appearing on the market for individual homeowners. A startup company in Australia, Lavo[16] now makes a cabinet in which water from your home supply is hydrolyzed by electricity from your solar panels during times when they are making excess power. This hydrogen is stored in a metal matrix as a hydride. When you need power,

16. http://www.lavo.com.au

the hydrogen is released and put into a fuel cell to make electricity. The unit is expensive, at $23,000, but it claims 40 kWh of storage and a life of 20,000 cycles, compared to only 13 kWh and 3,000 cycles for the Tesla Powerwall. Undoubtedly this technology will be further refined and come down in price in the future, thus providing more alternatives for people to be resilient in the area of their electricity.

Savings from this step that can be invested: The saving here can be substantial if your area is prone to power outages, which cause you to lose food because your refrigerator and freezer stop working. If your work or life is disrupted because of the lack of power, this also costs something. In addition, all your energy use from the grid can be programmed to be during off-peak hours.

LEVEL 6: TOTALLY OFF-GRID

This level is most appropriate if you are constructing a new house that is in a rural area some distance from the nearest existing utility poles. Bringing utility-provided electricity to your house in such a situation costs about $37 per foot or about $187,000 per mile.[17] This makes the cost of batteries and solar panels or wind turbines worth the expense. Otherwise, you are usually better off by going for Level 5.

More batteries are needed to be off-grid than at Level 5 because you must be prepared to support all of your day-to-day power needs for an extended period of cloudy days in the winter, not just for essential equipment like your refrigerator for a few days in an emergency. The Germans have a name for this situation—d*unkelflaute*, from *dunkel*, meaning

17. http://www.upgradedhome.com

dark, and *flaute* meaning a lull when there is no wind for wind generators. Germany has one or two weeks a year when it is very cloudy or foggy, with no wind, so their large investments in solar panels and wind turbines need some kind of very robust battery or fossil fuel generator backup.

In spite of the difficulties and expense of going off-grid, it has been estimated that between 180,000 and 250,000 people in the United States have done so.[18] It is a growing movement, with an increasing number of manufacturers catering to the need for specialized equipment.

Savings from this step that can be invested: Your entire energy bill can be put directly into savings in this case, as well as that part of your expenses saved due to use of an electric or plug-in hybrid vehicle.

Energy For Transportation: About 25% of all energy consumed in the world is used for transportation. About 63% of that is for personal transportation—getting you and your family and friends from one place to another, generally by automobile. Most of this transportation is powered by internal combustion engines using liquid fossil fuels, which an individual cannot make for himself. However, electric-powered vehicles are becoming more popular, and as seen above, we can indeed supply our own electricity. Methods of non-fossil fuel transportation include bicycles, electric bicycles, pedal/electric enclosed vehicles, and electric or plug-in hybrid cars. For a full treatment of these options, see Chapter 7: Transportation.

---

18. https://realestate.usnews.com/real-estate/articles/the-guide-to-off-grid-homes, https://offgridhack.com

. . .

Conclusion for Electrical Energy: The increasing popularity of off-grid houses shows that it is certainly possible to produce all the energy that a household needs from your own resources. In a rural area, there are many options. Even in a city, it is possible to produce most if not all of your own energy, if your cooking and house heating is all electric and you have room for a large solar array or another method of gathering energy.

Steps to Construct a Net Zero Energy House (new construction) in this order:

1. Design for passive solar heating and cooling, with thermal mass to smooth out the differences between day and night temperatures. (See Chapter 3.)

2. Design an efficient house "envelope" with R5 windows, R10 insulation below the slab, R20 in the walls below grade and R40 above it, and R80 insulation in your ceiling. These are well above the minimum required insulation in most building codes. After construction, photograph your house with an infrared camera on a cold day to see where heat is escaping and close those escape routes.

3. Install efficient electric heating and cooling, as needed, with a ground source heat pump if needed, and heat recovery ventilation if the climate is very cold in the winter. Install only LED lighting and energy efficient appliances.

4. When you have done the first three steps, only then install enough photo-voltaic panels or other generating equipment to power the needs of the house.

In other words, you get more "bang for your buck" if you economize your need for energy first and only then install enough solar panels (or other generating equipment) to cover the remaining need.

Bonus: Most of the activities discussed in this chapter are a benefit to the environment. If everyone moved up one or two levels of this chapter, we would go far in cleaning up our environment as well as eliminating any dependence on risky foreign sources of energy.

NEW DEVELOPMENTS TO WATCH FOR

- **New battery technology**, not only for electric cars (see Chapter 7) but also for homes for battery backup or for off-grid applications. Researchers are now working on plastic batteries that are larger per kWh than lithium ion, but would tolerate more cycles and would be significantly cheaper. Being physically larger or heavier is not a big problem for home applications, as compared to vehicles.
- More efficient **solar panels**.
- Solar panels embedded in roof shingles or wall elements.
- Transparent solar panels that can be used as windows.
- **New methods of harnessing wind power**. If these become cheap enough, they may allow wind power to be used in areas with low or erratic winds.

CHAPTER 2
ENERGY FOR COOKING AND HOT WATER

Devotees of raw food rely heavily on juicers and blenders, because otherwise they would have to spend as much time chewing as the chimps do. It is difficult, if not impossible, to extract sufficient energy from unprocessed plant matter to power a body with such a big, hungry brain.
Michael Pollan

I remember being shocked when I discovered some of my school pals didn't have books in their homes. I thought it was like not having oxygen, or hot water.
Iain Banks

Are You Resilient in Cooking? In the February 2021 freezing disaster in Texas, there were hundreds of thousands of people who could not cook a meal for up to a week because the electric grid and the natural gas distribution system both failed due to the unprecedented cold weather. Up to four million were without power at one point. What would you do if there were no electric power and no natural gas at your home for one day? For three days? For a week?

Since it was Texas, many of them were no doubt prepared to cook on their barbecues, although that would have had to be done outside in the freezing, snowy weather. One father cooked hot dogs and boiled water for coffee and hot chocolate on their outdoor wood-fired grill, since there was no power or other way to cook in their home, which was in the low 40s.[1]

Some that were even better prepared to at least heat up some water for tea or soup using their power banks (see the previous chapter). But even in normal times, there are ways that we can provide our own energy for cooking and at the same time be more resilient for difficult times.

As with all uses of energy, the more that people in a community are prepared to make their own energy for cooking, the more resilient the community is as a whole. They will not be dependent upon fossil fuel supplies, which will someday run out and, as we have seen, can be disrupted—and in the meantime, they cause pollution.

Self-produced energy for cooking can come from the following sources:

- solar oven
- wood (outside cooking): enclosed barbecue, rocket stove
- electric: grid-tied or off-grid solar or wind generator system
- biomass gas generator

All of these cooking sources, except for solar panels, are now or can easily be made domestically, so you are not hostage to supply chain problems.

---

1. https://www.youtube.com/watch?v=_dJK_u-lP38

LEVEL 1: SOLAR COOKERS, BARBECUES, ROCKET STOVES AND HAY BOXES

Solar Cookers: There are several designs of solar cookers. The simplest designs can be found on the internet and involve a cardboard box lined with aluminum foil that you angle toward the sun. Invest in a small, lightweight black pot with a lid, which you can place in the box, and you are set. A website with plans to make one is in Appendix 2.

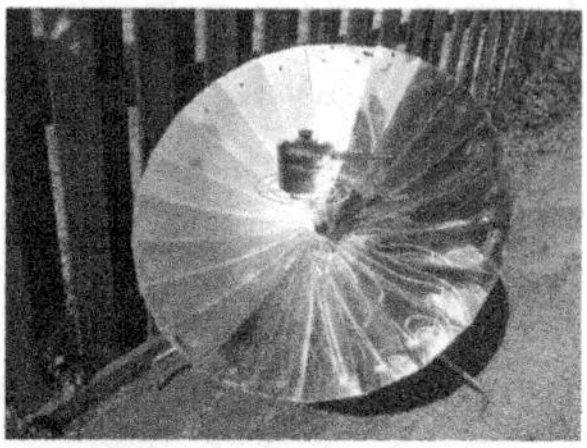

My folding parabolic solar cooker. It boils a cup of water in eight minutes, with an ambient air temperature of 69 F.

Another design involves a parabolic mirror with a platform at the focal point on which you place your black pot or pan, or a built-in container.

A variation on this is portable cooker shaped like half of a tube, made of reflective metal. At the focal point of the half-tube is a clear or dark colored tube where the food goes. Hot dogs, kebabs, or other long, thin food can be cooked inside this tube. If you are cooking at midday and there are no clouds, it can cook quickly with no fuel, fumes, or smoke. There are several examples of solar ovens in Appendix 2. Do not forget that solar cookers can be used indoors as well as outdoors if you have a window facing the sun.

https://gosun.co/collections/solar-ovens

Barbecues are familiar to everyone. If you cook using charcoal you have purchased, you are probably not saving any money or gaining any resilience compared with cooking on a propane stove. But if you use locally gathered wood, it will often cost you nothing and you will be using a renewable fuel, even though it does produce smoke and carbon dioxide. If you are in an urban area, you will have to be sensitive so as not to smoke out your neighbors. Do not use lumber that has been treated to make it resistant to rotting, or painted wood, because the smoke would then contain harmful chemicals.

You should also consider the difference between an **open fire** and a **closed fire**. When you use an open fire, like the barbecues usually found in public parks, you must allow the fire to die down to coals before cooking on it, so that your food is not burned in the flames. This stage of the fire can be attained much faster and use much less fuel if your barbecue has a lid with air openings on the top and the lower sides that can be controlled, like in the popular Weber barbecues or the circular, dome-shaped ceramic ones.

Start the wood fire and allow all the wood to become aflame. Then close the lid but keep the lower and upper openings mostly open. This allows enough oxygen to sustain coals, but not open flames. After a minute or two in this position, open the lid, place your food on the grill, and quickly close the lid again. Then after a few minutes, close the openings about halfway. Your food will cook, be smoked, and have good flavor, but you will save time, use much less wood, and create less smoke. Texas-style barbecues are also closed and are thus more efficient.

It is also possible to cook indoors using wood if you have a free-standing wood stove. Simply place a pot on top of the stove. This would only be appropriate during the winter when you were using the stove for heat.

Some older houses have indoor barbecue areas that are designed to use either charcoal or natural gas. My own home growing up had such an area. It was placed about four feet off the floor, so it was convenient to use while standing, and it vented into the same chimney as the fireplace, which was around the corner.

Tasty Wood: Some woods when burned impart a particularly tasty flavor to the food, including hickory (found in Eastern North America) and mesquite (native to Southwestern states). These types of wood are also dense and thus make a hotter fire. When your food has finished cooking, close all of the openings so that the fire is smothered. This will minimize the amount of smoke you emit, and save the resulting charcoal still in your barbecue for cooking your next meal. With this technique, you can cook a whole meal with very little wood fuel.

Rocket Stoves: You can also cook outside with pots and pans using wood. It is best to use cast iron cookware for this, which will last a long time and distribute the heat effectively. As with a barbecue, an enclosed fire will use your wood much more efficiently than an open fire. You can make such a stove yourself, using bricks or clay—there are instructions on the internet, and they are often called "rocket stoves" or "twig stoves." If you use bricks, red clay bricks will generally last longer, whereas concrete blocks can crack with the heat. See the videos about how to make these stoves yourself in Appendix 2. Lightweight versions of twig stoves can be purchased for backpacking—they start at about $25. They are likewise much more efficient than using an open fire.

Hay Boxes are insulated boxes that can allow food to finish cooking after you remove it from the heat source. In the old days, they were insulated with hay. You bring your food to boiling, cover it, and put the pot into the insulated box. There the food continues to cook. It will take slightly more time but will use quite a bit less fuel.

Savings from this step that can be invested: A modest amount of savings can be attained during the summer months by cooking with a barbecue or a solar cooker instead of your usual electric or gas range. In addition, by cooking outside, you do not heat up your house, thus reducing the load on your air conditioner.

LEVEL 2: SOLAR ELECTRIC

If you are at Level 4 or 5 with electricity production, then you can have an electric stove and your solar panels will be providing all the energy. The most efficient electric stove is the magnetic induction type. It is 5—10% more efficient than traditional electric heating coils, according to Consumer Reports.[2] This is because there is no heating element that must get hot first in order to transfer the heat to your pot. The magnetic system heats your pot directly, as long as your pot contains iron. Aluminum, copper, ceramic or glass pots will not work, unfortunately, and it is often hard to know which metal pots contain iron just by looking at them or feeling their weight. To know which pots will work, simply use a magnet. If it sticks to the bottom of the pot, you can use it. As a bonus, since the stove top is not heated, it is easily cleaned, and children will not burn their fingers as readily.

If you power your cooking in this way, you are self-sufficient and resilient! Another bonus: You will not be putting the products of combustion into your house air to breathe, as with a gas stove.

Savings from this step that can be invested: A significant

2. https://www.consumerreports.org/appliances/ranges/pros-and-cons-of-induction-cooktops-and-ranges-a5854942923/

amount of your bill for natural gas or propane can be eliminated by this step.

LEVEL 3: BIOGAS DIGESTER, WOOD STOVE FOR COOKING

If you now use propane or electricity from the grid for cooking and live in a rural area in a part of the country that has warm weather most of the time, you can invest in a biomass digester (generator). This is a special, large, heavy-duty plastic bag into which you put any organic material—kitchen scraps, lawn and tree clippings, fallen leaves, and even animal droppings. Anything organic that will break down easily will work, so large bones and fruit pits are not useful here. Air is kept out of the bag. Bacteria that thrive in the absence of oxygen eat this organic matter and convert it into methane, one of the main components of natural gas. A hose connects the top of the bag to your house to your stove where you can burn it. Pressure is supplied simply by a weight on top of the bag since high pressure is not needed.

As a bonus, a liquid collects at the bottom of the bag and is drawn off through a pipe and valve. It is an excellent fertilizer. You can invest in ready-made biogas kits for about $720 (see Appendix 2). If you are handy with making things, instructions for making your own biogas generator are available on YouTube and elsewhere on the internet. Such a generator will pay for itself very quickly and also make you more resilient.

This option for making energy is for warmer climates because the warmer the bag, the better the bacteria work, and, in any case, the bag should be kept at an average temperature of 68 degrees or more. Thus, it works best if it is kept in a sunny greenhouse, even though the digestion process creates some of its own heat. Usually, the bags are black or a dark color for this reason.

This simple technology is also being used by communities. My own city has an industrial-sized biodigester that utilizes all the organic ("green") waste collected in the city. The methane produced is used to generate electricity—enough to power 600 homes (6.2 million kilowatt hours per year), according to the city. The digester produces compost and liquid fertilizer as well, which are used by surrounding farms. If this green waste were simply added to a landfill, it would still decompose to create methane, but the gas would just be wasted, escaping into the atmosphere to become a contributor to global warming.

Small, simple versions of these digesters are being produced for use in developing countries, particularly in Africa and southern Asia where it is always warm. See the links in Appendix 2 for this chapter. Then people no longer have to cook over smoky open fires, using firewood or charcoal collected from far distances and contributing to rampant deforestation.

A large portable version of this method is now available, called the "Power Pallet."[3] It combines a stainless steel biogas digester with an electric generator that runs on the gas, producing 25, 50, or 130 kW of electricity. The 25 kW version needs 1 kilogram of bio material for each kWh of energy produced and costs about $50,000. It is somewhat noisy, producing 75 dB measured 7 meters away. Naturally, this is for remote sites with lots of plant waste that need a lot of electrical energy for relatively short periods of time. There are options to capture the heat energy produced by the unit, which, like all biogas generators, also produces fertilizer.

Also at this level, if you are in a rural area with access to

---

3. https://www.allpowerlabs.com/pp30-power-pallet

wood, it could make sense to install a **wood-fired cooking stove**. There are "pot-bellied" stoves with only one burner or full-sized stoves complete with ovens like the ones that our ancestors used a hundred years ago. These are not cheap and require roof work for the chimney, which is why they are at Level 3. If you live in a warm climate and the heat generated by such a stove would be unwanted inside your home, then consider creating an outdoor kitchen—a patio with a roof but no walls where your cooking could be done.

Savings from this step that can be invested: The savings would be significant in any case, but could be substantial if you are now using propane that is delivered to your home.

ENERGY FOR HOT WATER

Hot water inside your house is one of the hallmarks of a modern dwelling. It consumes about 17% of the energy used in the average home. Sources of this energy available to the self-reliant investor include solar and wood. Like the sources for cooking, all of these are now or can be made easily in North America, and are not subject to supply chain difficulties.

LEVEL 1: CAMPING

There is no entry-level way to create your own hot water for your home. But if you are camping, you can invest in a solar shower bag, which would replace heating water for bathing on your camp stove. It is black or dark colored, with a filling hole and a short hose with a shower head. You fill it and place it in the sun. To take a shower, you hang it from a tree and the water flows by gravity. There are various sizes available, from 1 to 10 gallons. A 10-gallon one even has a thermometer built in and costs only $18. The manufacturers claim that the water will be ready for a shower (113 degrees F) in three hours.[4]

For car camping, you can buy a long black PVC plastic tube about 4-6 inches in diameter that you close at both ends and attach to the roof rack of your vehicle. Install a filling cap on the top, and a fitting for a hose and shower head on the bottom. When the water is warmed by the sun, you open a valve and water flows by gravity. This is particularly useful for surfers, scuba divers, or spearfishers who park in isolated areas, so they can wash off after their session. Ready-made units can be purchased that can be pressurized to provide a faster flow of water (see Appendix 2).

Savings from this step that can be invested: If you like to go camping and would otherwise heat up water on a camp stove for washing, then you will save some money here.

LEVEL 2: SOLAR HOT WATER FOR YOUR HOUSE

The simplest system for solar hot water involves a tank on your roof with a black solar hot water panel beneath it, angled toward the sun. Water in the black panel is heated by the sun, and naturally rises up through a pipe to the top of the tank. Cooler water from the bottom of the tank goes through another pipe down to the bottom of the panel. Another pipe goes from the middle of the tank down into the house to be used in the bathrooms and kitchen. No water

4. https://www.amazon.com/RISEPRO-gallons-Heating-Temperature-Climbing/dp/B01L3N2U3M/ref=asc_df_B01L3N2U3M

pumps of any kind are needed because the water circulates from the tank to the panel and back by natural convection.

From my own personal observation, nearly all houses in the Eastern Mediterranean region, including southern Turkey, Syria, Lebanon, Cyprus, Jordan, Israel, and Palestine have hot water using this kind of system.

In my own photo on the right, from Cyprus, you can see a large white fresh water tank on top, and underneath a smaller stainless steel hot water tank. Below that tank are two solar hot water panels. These are on top of an apartment building in which each apartment (condo) has its own solar hot water system on the common roof.

Solahart, a company that started in sunny Australia, has been selling this type of unit there and in North America for decades, but other companies are now selling them as well. Many models and sizes are available, and some models account for climates where the unit would be subject to freezing temperatures. Systems sold in Australia and North America usually have an electric heating element in the tank for backup. They come with either flat plate collectors, which are long-lasting and durable but more expensive, or evacuated tube collectors which are less durable but heat faster and are cheaper.

Example: During the Great Depression, my mother lived in a house that had no indoor bathroom. During the winter they bathed in a portable metal tub inside, filled from pots on the stove. But during most of the year, they used an outdoor shower, made from a black metal water barrel mounted on top of a wooden shower stall. The sun heated the water in the barrel, which flowed by gravity down through a valve and shower head.

A variation of the simple system is called an "active" solar hot water system and is particularly used in cooler climates. A solar hot water panel sits on your roof. Water from this unit is pumped down to a tank inside the house, where it can keep warm on cold days. Alternatively, the panel on the roof has a special liquid that is pumped down to the hot water tank and warms the tank through a heat exchanger. The special liquid absorbs heat readily and will not freeze during cold winter nights.

Wood-fired Hot Water: In off-grid situations far from civilization in a cold climate, it is also possible to design a water heating system using the heat from a fireplace or wood-fired stove. A tube with water circles the chimney pipe and heats the nearby water tank. Water flows from the tank by gravity.

HELPING YOUR COMMUNITY

As with alternative methods of providing electricity, alternative hot water systems help the community as well as the individual. They reduce the reliance of the community on nonrenewable resources, which often come from politically volatile regions of the world and can also add greenhouse gases to the atmosphere. Even though North America is self-sufficient in natural gas, it comes at an environmental cost both to obtain it and to burn it, so if we can use other methods to achieve the same result (hot water), it is better.

Savings from this step that can be invested: If you have gas hot water, then a substantial amount of your gas or propane goes for hot water. This would be saved.

NEW DEVELOPMENTS TO WATCH FOR

- Even more portable and more **efficient solar cookers**.
- **New designs of solar water heaters** that are less obtrusive and fit more easily with any type of roof architecture.

CHAPTER 3
HEATING AND COOLING YOUR HOUSE

If I close my eyes, I can remember the first apartment where I lived with my family in Newark, N.J., in the late 1930s. The rooms were lined up like train cars—you had to go through one to get to another—and there wasn't any heat or hot water.

Frankie Valli

It was luxuries like air conditioning that brought down the Roman Empire. With air conditioning their windows were shut, they couldn't hear the barbarians coming.

Garrison Keillor

What Would You Do? The biggest problem during the Texas ice storm of February 2021 was heating houses and apartments for the week when there was no electricity or gas in many areas. Many homes were in the 50s F inside, and some were near freezing. This caused the water pipes of many houses to freeze and burst. What would you do to keep warm if there was no electricity or natural gas supply to your house for a week during the winter? Do not forget that most homes that are heated by natural gas also require electricity to ignite the gas and to power fans to distribute the heat around the house. Only those homes with old-fashioned wall or floor heaters with pilot lights would still have have gas heat if the electricity were out.

Between 50% and 70% of the energy used in homes is used for heating, ventilating, and air conditioning (HVAC), depending on your climate zone. This is because changing the temperature of an entire home requires much more energy than your refrigerator, cooking, or lighting. The last item in particular takes much less energy now than it used to, due to more efficient light bulbs being available today. But there have not been comparable advances in heating and cooling, until recently.

The best way to heat or cool your house is not to let it get too hot or cold in the first place. This involves proper insulation and the use of thermal mass. Insulation keeps the extreme cold or heat out of your house. A thermal mass is a heavy item inside your house that will retain heat or coolness and moderate any swings between day and night. In inland areas, particularly deserts, the difference between day and night temperatures can be 40 degrees F (22 C) or more. A thermal mass can absorb and retain the comfortable temperature and slowly release it later.

ALTERNATIVES

In most cases, systems to allow you to maintain your house at a comfortable temperature must be built into the house when it is constructed. Methods for collecting **heat energy** include:

- passive solar heating
- active solar heating
- earth heat (also called geothermal)
- wood stove
- electric heat (using solar panels or wind or hydroelectric generator, from Chapter 1)

Heat is measured in British Thermal Units (BTUs). The cost of 1 million BTUs according to one researcher is the following:[1]

- natural gas $8.24
- hardwood $13.89
- kerosene $19.17
- heating oil $19.73
- wood pellets $20.96
- propane $23.12
- electricity $32.24

These prices depend a lot on the availability of these sources and prices in your region, and your own particular situation. Heating oil is available in the eastern parts of North America, but not in the west. Wood may not be readily available on the Great Plains. Natural gas is only available in urban areas with gas lines. The prices are given so we can see the general relative price of these different sources, although the absolute prices go up and down with the market.

Cooling can be as necessary to life as heating. Every year some elderly people die due to becoming overheated in their dwelling that is either not air conditioned during a heat

1. https://extension.okstate.edu/fact-sheets/true-cost-of-energy-comparisons-apples-to-apples.html

wave or there is a power outage. For example, in 2021 after Hurricane Ida hit New Orleans and knocked out power, at least five elderly people died due to the lack of air conditioning.[2]

Traditional air conditioning is actually a type of heat management. You are transferring heat from an inside space to the outside. The transferring of heat, like the generation of heat, requires much more energy than lighting or simply blowing air. But there are other ways of managing heat other than transferring it to the outside. Ways of heat management include:

- evaporative cooling
- passive cooling (solar chimneys and wind towers)
- earth cooling
- absorption cooling using a heat source
- traditional electric refrigeration using a compressor

As with other uses of energy, the more that each individual in a community conserves energy or provides their own through alternative means, the more resilient the community is as a whole. It should also be noted that nearly all the items in this chapter are produced in North America and are thus not subject to international supply chain difficulties.

LEVEL 1: TEMPERATURE MONITORING, SOLAR GAIN, EVAPORATIVE COOLER

Temperature Monitoring: A first step toward controlling

---

2. https://weather.com/news/news/2021-09-17-hurricane-ida-low-income-senior-housing-heat-evacuations

the temperature of your dwelling is to know the temperature both inside and out at a glance. Invest in an indoor/outdoor thermometer, and place it on the north side of the inside of your house, or in a place so that the outdoor sensor is not in the sun. This will tell you when it would be advantageous to open your windows. In the summer, open your windows as soon as the temperature outside drops below the level inside, and in the winter, do the opposite. This handy gadget is not expensive.

This is my own unit.

Heating: Use Solar Gain: Open your south-facing drapes and blinds during the winter to allow the sun to heat the inside. Try to place solid, heavy, dark-colored items in this sunny area, such as decorative black rocks or dark-colored bricks, so the maximum amount of energy is absorbed.

Cooling: If your climate is very hot in the summer, then changing your lights from incandescent or CFL to LEDs will have a double benefit. You will spend less for the energy to run them, and the LEDs will add less heat to your house that you have to get rid of.

You can also cook outside during the hot months on a BBQ. If you would normally cook something on your stove, consider plugging in an electric hot plate outside. Why heat up your house by cooking indoors?

If you live in a dry climate, you could try one of the small "air coolers" that use water to cool the air. They will not work effectively in humid climates, like the Gulf Coast, but would work in the deserts of California through West Texas. They cost between $29 and $45 for a small, personal one (four stars on Amazon), or about $110 for one that will cool a room. In the old days in the desert, they made "swamp coolers" that would cool the whole house in this way. Most of these have been replaced by refrigerated air conditioners in recent decades, but in dry climates they are much more economical than air conditioning systems that use refrigeration.

Savings from this step that can be invested: This step can save you a little (for an indoor/outdoor thermometer) to a lot (for an evaporative cooler in place of an air conditioner).

LEVEL 2: MEDIUM-LEVEL UPGRADING OF AN EXISTING HOUSE.

Double pane windows, other conservation, wood-burning stoves, whole-house fans, and solar greenhouses

Windows: At this level, you should invest in double-glazed (double pane), low-e windows, if your house does not already have them. If you live in a region that gets either very cold or very hot, you might even install triple or quadruple glazing, especially if you have any windows that face north (in the northern hemisphere) in a cold climate. Put heavy drapes and/or double-thickness shades on all windows, since it is the windows that allow most of your heat to escape in the winter and enter during a hot summer. Make sure that the shades cover the entire window from side to side and top to bottom, with no gaps.

. . .

Example of single vs double pane windows: Our house, located in an area with 40–50 degree F swings between day and night during the summer, was built in the early 1970s and originally had single pane, aluminum frame windows, common at that time. If we closed our windows in the morning, when the outside air temperature rose higher than inside, the temperature inside would remain up to 20 degrees cooler for a number of hours. That is, about noon, the temperature could be 90 degrees outside but still only 70 inside.

After the installation of double-glazed windows with plastic frames, the difference could be as much as 30 degrees. It would often be 100 degrees outside, but only 70 inside at noon without air conditioning. In the winter, there was also a noticeable improvement in heat retention, as well as the elimination of condensation on the inside of the windows. As a bonus, double-glazed windows also work much better in keeping out noise, such as from a busy street or nearby highway.

Wall Coverings: In the Middle Ages, the walls of castles were covered by tapestries. This was not just for decoration —it was to add an insulating layer between the cold stone walls and the room. You can do this with an existing house today to improve your insulation, particularly on a wall facing north (in the northern hemisphere). A quilt or any kind of padded cloth will do.

Wood Heating: If your house has a traditional open fireplace, be aware that having an open fire there in the winter may add to the ambiance, but it does not warm the house. In fact, it actually cools it overall because nearly all the heat from the fire goes up the chimney. That air is replaced by air coming in under the doors and around the windows from the outside, which is probably cold. You feel warmer when you are near the fire, but the parts of your house away from the fire become colder. The traditional fireplace in many North American homes was originally designed long ago for cooking, not heating. It was made so that if you were cooking in that fireplace during the summer, the heat would *not* stay in the house, but go outside through the chimney.

To use a fireplace to actually heat the house, you must invest in a **fireplace insert**, which costs about $1,200 and up. One important feature of this item is a door on the firebox with a window that allows heat to radiate into the room and also allows you to see what is going on inside. The other important feature is the ability to regulate how much air from your house enters the burning chamber. When you start the fire, this regulator is all the way open, so that the fire can get going. Once all the large pieces are in flames, you begin to close down this regulator, so that there are no longer large flames, but the wood is glowing red. This lets a minimum amount of hot air go up the chimney, and a maximum amount of heat radiate into your room. It also slows down the burning so that once you fill it with wood, it will burn for many hours without further attention.

A poorly made stove will burn the wood too quickly, forcing you to feed it often, thus disrupting your day, wasting wood, and creating unnecessary smoke. Most inserts also have an electric fan that circulates air from the room to behind the burning chamber and out the top back into your room, so that your fireplace is even more efficient. These inserts can be installed in nearly any open fireplace.

A cheaper version of the fireplace insert consists of a

series of parallel tubes that replace the grate to hold the wood. A fan takes air from the room and blows it through the tubes and back out into the room. This system is only marginally effective, from my own experience. It does indeed blow hot air into the room, but because the fire is open, it uses the wood very quickly, and a majority of the heat still goes up the chimney.

If you live in a colder climate, outside of cities where fireplace burning may be prohibited, and have access to free or low-cost firewood from dead trees and branches, this will definitely be a wise investment in your resilience. If you live in such an area but do not have a fireplace in your house already, consider investing in a **free-standing wood stove**. They can be even more efficient than an insert in a built-in fireplace because the unit will heat all the air surrounding it, as well as the air surrounding the chimney tube going up to the ceiling. Free-standing wood stoves come in many sizes—some are even small enough to install in a trailer or motor home. Not all wood-burning stoves are the same—do research to determine which one is the most efficient for the money.

Using dead trees and branches for heating serves another purpose as well. Many forests are full of such material, creating a big fire hazard. Removing this material reduces the potential for huge conflagrations that threaten whole communities.

If you are in a cold winter climate and heating with a wood stove often, you will want to get one that includes **secondary burning** or has a **catalytic converter**. A stove with secondary burning has a pipe with many holes in it across the upper part of the firebox that adds air and thus burns the gases that come out of the wood. This not only burns cleaner, but adds to the heat you obtain. A stove with a catalytic converter has a special substance in the upper part of the firebox that burns the wood exhaust, just like the catalytic converter on a car. There is a lever that allows exhaust to bypass the converter until it gets hot enough to function. Some urban areas only allow wood stoves if they have this feature because they produce the least amount of smoke out the chimney. An added bonus of catalytic converters is that since no extra air is being added (like with a secondary burn system), the fire will burn longer. However, if you like to relax while watching the flames dancing in your stove, then the secondary burn system would be better, since the catalytic converter system lets the wood smolder rather then burn with flames.

For a free-standing fireplace, you can also invest in a small fan with a thermo-electrically powered motor. You set this on top of the fireplace. When the metal there becomes hot, the difference between this hot surface and the cooler air some inches above generates a small electrical current, which powers the fan to circulate the warm air into your room. The fans cost about $40. It is a handy gadget because it only comes on when the stove is hot, which is when you need it, and there are no wires to get burned or batteries to replace.

Wood fuel must be dry—that is, not newly cut and green. Wood stove manufacturers advise that the wood you burn should contain less than 20% moisture. To determine this, obtain a firewood moisture tester costing between $18 and $35. It uses two probes and a small electrical current to determine the moisture content. Green wood takes at least a year to dry, depending on the climate, so you must plan ahead.

The harder (denser and heavier) the wood, the longer any given size log will burn. The most numerous hardwoods in North America include oak, maple, beech, alder, poplar, ash, cherry, and hickory. Softer woods include pine, fir, hemlock, spruce, larch, and cedar. If you have a choice, try to find harder wood to burn.

Fireplace Insert Example: We lived in an area where winter temperatures were often below freezing, and sometimes as low as 18 degrees F. We installed a fireplace insert after an earthquake damaged the chimney, and we had to do some repair work on the fireplace anyway. The first winter after the installation, natural gas (primarily used by us for home heating) prices went up by 20%, but our bill decreased by 20%. All the wood we burned came from dead branches from our own property and lumber scraps from construction projects, and so cost us nothing.

Another wood heating design is known as a "**rocket mass heater**." By drawing the hot gasses through a metal "heat riser" or "heating barrel" and then through a horizontal bench made of adobe or cob, the maximum amount of heat is utilized. Unlike traditional wood stoves, it uses a vertical, gravity-powered self-feeding design that burns small sticks rather than large logs, but a more traditional horizontal fuel feeding area can also work. It also can be used for cooking. However, since much of it is made of clay or adobe, it is hard to add to an existing house. After the fire has gone out, it continues to warm the house for several days. Therefore, rocket mass heaters are best for climates with a long, cold winter.

Burning wood for heat is not ecologically clean, but it is renewable, you can provide it yourself from your own property, and it may cost you very little money. Using a modern closed fireplace with a catalytic chamber is the most efficient way to use this renewable resource. To help the environment, do not cut down live trees just to use for firewood. Instead, if possible, use dead trees and branches and pieces of lumber left over from construction projects. But if you must grow your own firewood, then choose trees for your climate that can be cut and then grow back from the stumps. They will grow much faster than trees grown from seedlings, since they will already have a good root system.

Another way to burn wood is to use **wood pellets**. However, if you buy a pellet stove, you are locked into burning only pellets, which you must purchase, thus decreasing your resilience. Even if you buy wood rather than collect it free, wood is cheaper than pellets, as the chart at the beginning of the chapter shows. Some pellets are made from the tops and branches of trees harvested for paper or lumber, which is a good use of what would otherwise be wasted. But an increasing percentage of pellets being sold today is made from trees cut down only to make pellets. This does not help the environment or the overall resilience of society. Pellet stoves also require electricity to run the device that feeds the pellets into the burning chamber at the rate you desire. Therefore, if your power goes out, you will not have any heat from this kind of stove.

If you use a wood stove or fireplace insert, you may wonder what you can do with the ashes. First of all, they can be used as compost in your garden—see Chapter 4: Resilient Sources of Food. In addition to helping the soil, ashes also repel some garden pests. Secondly, ashes can be used to clean up oil stains on concrete, since they readily absorb liquids. They also have an abrasive quality, which makes ashes good for cleaning the inside of the glass in your insert or wood stove. In snowy climates, they make an excellent snow removal material for walks or driveways. Finally, some companies are using ash to make bricks. This might be difficult on an individual basis, but it is something to consider.

Solar Greenhouse: The heat gain of your existing house can be improved by adding a greenhouse on the south side. Make sure that the greenhouse is attached to the house without any gaps. To increase its efficiency, put black or dark-colored material along the wall of the house inside the greenhouse, where the sun can shine on it. Include vents that can be opened or closed, so that the greenhouse does not become too hot in the summer, but helps to heat your house in the winter.

Cooling—Whole House Fan: If you live in an area that is hot during the day but cools off at night, then invest in a whole-house fan. Turn it on in the evening when it cools down, and this will take the hot air from near your ceiling and convey it outside through your attic. Then cooler air from your windows, which can be cracked open (and secured with a stick or other device), will come in to replace it. This is particularly useful if you live in an urban area where it might not be safe to leave your windows wide open all night. If you do not want to leave your windows open even a crack during the night, then install vents in your floor (or in the wall near the floor if your house is built on a slab) connected to the outside with a short pipe. Make sure that there is a way to close these vents during the winter. You also want to make sure that such vents do not become a way for insects to enter your home.

. . .

Passive Cooling: A passive way to cool your house involves a "cooling tower." These were a standard feature in some parts of the Middle East in past centuries. In a central part of the house, there is a small, high place—two or three stories high, but only 4-6 feet in diameter. At the top of this area there is an opening for air to go out. Hot air from the house rises into this tower and goes out, replaced by cooler air from areas outside. This cooler air can come in by several routes. In desert regions, air near the ground is heated by the sun, and can be more than 150 degrees F. In contrast, air 6 to 10 feet off the ground is much cooler. Therefore, there is an opening near the roof in the direction of the prevailing wind that catches those breezes, and directs them down and into the house. Before the air enters the house, it could flow through a damp filter, as in the diagram below, or over a pool of water, which would cool it.

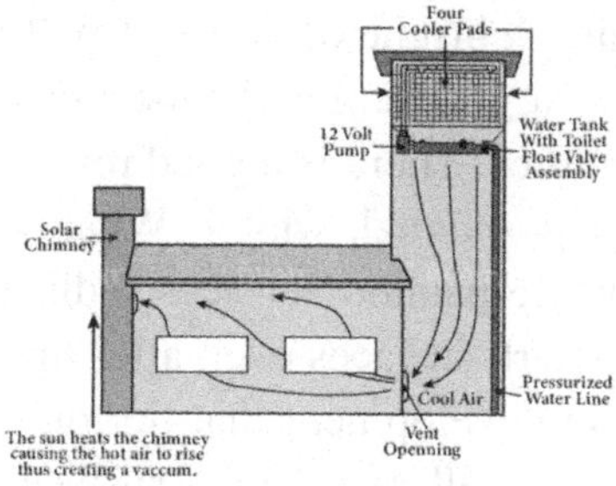

Diagram by arafat_creative through fiverr.com

If you are remodeling a house, take advantage of the designs that would contribute to a cooler house during the summer. Avoid windows facing east or especially west, where they would let in light and heat during hot summer afternoons. Put overhangs over south-facing windows that would be large enough to shade the house during the summer, when the sun is high.

Most importantly, do not let overhangs be so large as to shade your windows during the winter when the sun will be low in the sky and you will want its warmth. In some cases, a retractable awning might be a good solution. If you plant trees on the south side of the house, make them deciduous, so that they lose their leaves in the winter and let the sun in, but will shade your house during the summer. Put evergreen trees on the east, north, and west sides to protect the house from cold north winds in the winter.

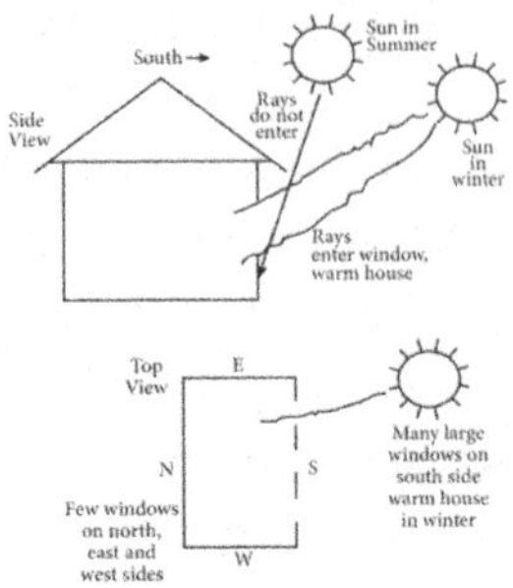

Color Matters: Lighter colors reflect the sun's rays, and prevent heat gain. A bright white paint will reflect the most heat, and thus be a good color for locations subject to high summer temperatures. There is a good reason why houses on Greek islands are painted white! What is not generally known is that white-painted surfaces radiate heat back into space more than dark surfaces even after the sun goes down. Paints are now in development that not only reflect most of the sun's rays, but will result in a surface that is a lower temperature than the ambient air even while the sun is shining on it.

In the same way, dark colors absorb the sun's rays. If your location needs more heating in the winter than cooling in the summer, then dark colors for your house may be in order. Hopefully, in the future there may be paint that can change color depending on the season, or perhaps change its sun-absorbing qualities without changing apparent color.

. . .

Heating with electricity powered by solar panels: As related in Chapter 1, we have a grid-tied solar panel setup, and during the winter of 2022—2023 we heated our house with electric space heaters powered by our solar panels instead of our gas furnace. Bills for natural gas in our area tripled, whereas ours stayed low—only $25 for the month of January. The previous January we paid $75, so our bill would have been about $225 had we continued to use gas for heat. At our annual "true up" payment for electricity, we paid $13, which included the energy we used for space heating.

Savings from this step that can be invested: Since a large amount of energy is used for HVAC in the average home, the savings for this step can be in the hundreds of dollars monthly in very hot or very cold climates.

LEVEL 3: BUILDING A NEW HOUSE WITH PASSIVE SOLAR DESIGN

If you are building a new house, or extensively remodeling an older one, make sure that it is done with conservation and passive heating and cooling principles in mind, so that you build resilience into your house. These principles are:

1. Super-insulated envelope—three times the usual regulations, particularly in a climate that is either extremely hot or cold. Old houses typically have R12 insulation in the walls, and newer homes have R24. Strive to have R70 in severe climates. With the siding, this means that your walls will be 2 feet thick. This is especially important on the north walls of houses in cold climates, and on the south and west facing walls in hot climates (in the northern hemisphere).

2. Minimize thermal bridging, which is any solid structural element that directly connects the outside with the

inside of the house. Instead, have insulation everywhere between the outside and the inside. In traditional building methods with 2x4 lumber, every 2x4 in the wall of the house is a thermal bridge. Walls will necessarily be thicker to allow for insulated framing. Window frames will also be constructed so as not to be thermal bridges.

3. Airtight construction—taking care to have no air leaks around doors or windows.

4. Heat recovery ventilation. Every heating and air conditioning system takes a certain amount of air from the outside, so that you are not breathing the same air all the time. In severe climates, this outside air could be very cold or very hot. A heat exchanging system will recover up to 75% of the heat (or cold) in the air that goes out, and transfer it to the incoming fresh air.

5. High-performance glazing—this means at least double, and in many cases triple pane windows.

6. Orientation of the house and windows. Houses are usually rectangular. If at all possible, the long sides should face south and north, rather than east and west. This way, the house can absorb the maximum amount of winter sun, and avoid the long hot afternoon sun in the summer coming from the west. Put more and larger windows facing south (in the northern hemisphere), and fewer and smaller, if any, windows on the north side, especially in colder climates.

Passive solar means that there are no moving parts. You simply allow the sun to shine into the house during the winter and fall on dark-colored, solid, massive surfaces, such as a cement or rock floor or wall, that can absorb a lot of heat during the day. This floor must be isolated from the ground by insulation so that the energy it collects radiates from the floor into your house and not into the ground. This floor is a thermal mass, which takes a long time to gain or lose heat. See below under Thermal Mass. For more information on passive houses, visit the website of the Passive House Institute, given in Appendix 2 under Chapter 3.

Your house should reflect "vernacular design"—that is, it should fit the specific climate and site where it is built and take advantage of local materials and craftsmanship. This way it will be most efficient and allow the inhabitants to be the most resilient.

A passive solar house does not mean that your house must look like it landed from outer space, or be out of character with your neighbors. It may look only slightly different. New solar roofing tiles are now being produced so that solar electric panels will not be visible, if you don't want them to be. High-quality insulation can be part of any shape or design of house. However, consider this: The most popular hybrid vehicle is the Toyota Prius. Could it be that part of its popularity is because it *does* look different from non-hybrid cars? Could this be an indication of the resale value of a house that looked like it was energy efficient?

Heating: Even in very cold northern climates, 80-100% of the heating load can be done by the sun, as shown by people living with passive solar homes in Wisconsin and Canada.[3] The "Earthship" designs of Mike Reynolds, who lives in Taos, New Mexico, at an altitude of almost 7,000 feet, are another example—see the links in Appendix 2 for this chapter and for Chapter 6. His designs involve a large earth berm on the north, east, and west sides of the house, providing a large thermal mass. There are no windows on these sides. The south side is all windows, through which the winter sun warms and lights the interior. All the necessary

3. A net zero energy use house in upstate New York can be seen here: https://www.youtube.com/watch?v=QrF_-uNcFlg

heating in an Earthship house is provided by passive solar design, although in very cold climates most of them have a wood stove as backup. For more on Earthship houses, see the end of Chapter 6: Water.

Example: A friend of mine was building a house near Almaty, Kazakhstan, which is located at 43 degrees north latitude, and an altitude of 3,000 feet. The climate is continental, with snow on the ground for about three months every winter, and warm summers. I visited him as he was installing bricks for the foundation wall, and asked him where the windows were going to be. "Here and here," he said, indicating places on the eastern, northern, and western walls. I advised him to put a large window facing south so the winter sun would heat the house. As an added bonus, it would provide a view towards the beautiful Tien Shan mountain range, with peaks going up to 16,000 feet. Later, after his house was finished and he had lived in it for a year, he thanked me for my advice on window placement, saying that the large window facing south really helped to warm the house in the winter.

Another form of passive solar design involves a shallow black box with a glass cover, mounted in a south-facing wall. Air from the house enters at the bottom, is warmed in the black metal box, and exits back into the house from the top by natural convection without fans. One company sells ready-made units like this for about $470 that put out 750 W (2500 BTU) of heat.[4] They would not be difficult to make yourself. You would make it to sit below a south-facing window, which you would open just enough to install the air tubes going out to the unit and back in. Of course, you could

4. https://www.arcticasolar.com/products/750-series-solar-air-heater

also drill holes in a south-facing wall for this purpose, but this would be more complicated. They would be very useful in an off-grid situation, and in places of a building where you might not want windows on the south-facing wall for some reason. Some use thermal convection to move the air from the room to the heater and back, but others use a small fan. There is a link to a video to make your own in Appendix 2.

Any of the above passive systems would have saved the people of Texas who endured indoor temperatures as low as the 30s during the February 2021 cold weather disaster. A passive solar house might have dropped to the low 60s due to the lack of sunshine during part of that week but would not have fallen lower due to better insulation and more thermal mass.

A type of **semi-passive solar design** was used in a house in Atascadero, California, constructed by architecture students at California Polytechnic University San Luis Obispo.[5] The roof contains a large water bag, like a water bed. In the winter, the cover over this bag is retracted during the day, allowing the sun to heat the water. In the evening, the cover is put back over the bag, and the heat gathered during the day radiates into the house. In the summer, when the house needs to be cooled, the process is reversed—open during the night and closed during the day. The disadvantage of this design is that the house had to be constructed very sturdily (and thus expensively) to hold up the heavy water bag. I call it semi-passive because a large roof section must move using motors twice a day.

Active solar heating is any solar heating system that requires blowers or pumps to move the heat into the house. A house can be constructed that has solar hot water heaters on the roof. During the day, this water is pumped down to a

5. http://www.solarmirror.com/cgi-bin/faq.cgi?file=30

large tank under the house. In the evening when the heat is needed, this water is then pumped to radiators inside. Alternately, heat is collected by air in black-painted boxes on the roof and stored in large rocks in a room under the house. When the heat is needed, other blowers direct air from this chamber into the living area. This is naturally much more complicated and expensive than passive systems.

If you have electric heat, a heat pump is more efficient than resistance heat, such as a portable heater with an electric resistance coil. If your climate is very cold in the winter, you might consider a geothermal heat pump, also called a ground source heat pump. This requires pipes with special fluid running in a large loop, about 6 feet underground, depending on how deep frost goes in your area. These pipes tap into the latent temperature of the ground, which in temperate climates is about 55 degrees F. It transfers that heat energy to the house through a heat exchanger, resulting in a savings of 75% compared with standard heating coils. This system is becoming very popular in Sweden, a country that has severe winters.

The same system can work in reverse during hot summer months, with savings of 20-40% over a traditional air conditioner. The disadvantage is the large area this requires (about 1 acre) and much expensive digging. However, a variant of this system uses vertical rather than horizontal tubes, put into a drilled hole. If you have the machinery to do this yourself, it may be worth your while. Tax credits may be available.

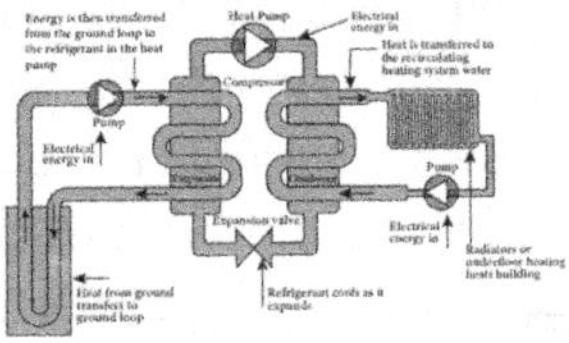

Diagram by arafat_creative through fiverr.com

. . .

Geothermal Cooling: If you live in a climate that is hot during the day but cools off at night, then you could invest in simple air tubes that use a fan to bring in cool air from an underground area around or under your house. If you have ever visited a cave, such as Carlsbad Caverns in New Mexico, you have experienced this firsthand. Although the caverns are in a desert area, the air inside the caverns is a constant 55 degrees F. In a geothermal cooling system, the tubes have to be at least 20 to 30 feet long and placed at least 6 feet under the surface. The longer the tubes and the farther under the ground they are buried, the better they will work. This is much simpler than the heat pump mentioned above, and they are used in Earthship house designs.

However, before embarking on this kind of project, be sure to test your site for the presence of radon gas. This is an odorless and colorless radioactive gas that is naturally present in the soil of some regions of the world, including parts of North America. Air tubes running underground would pick up this gas and carry it into your living space. High or long-duration exposure to radon gas can lead to lung and other types of cancer. Radon tests are readily available and are not expensive. You must leave a small open box in the target area for about a week and then send it in to a lab, and they will notify you of the result. To get a general idea of the prevalence of radon in your area, there are tables of tests that have already been done in every state and county available online. Radon can also be a problem for houses built on a slab, rather than on a raised foundation since the gas can percolate up through the concrete slab.

Thermal Mass: If the average outside temperature of day and night in your area is in a comfortable range, then it would help your comfort to have a large thermal mass as part of the walls of the house such as brick, rocks, or earth. For example, our apartment in Central Asia had brick walls fully 2 feet thick. The heating system was run by the city and was turned on in the fall on a certain date and off on a certain date in the spring, regardless of the weather. Sometimes, there was a cold snap or even snow after the time when the system was shut off. But because the walls were 2 feet thick, it took at least four days for that cold to go through them. By then, usually, the cold snap was over. The average annual temperature for your city can be found on the internet.

If the average outside temperature is either too hot or too cold for comfort, then a thermal mass that is connected to this outside temperature will hinder your comfort inside the home. Therefore, your thermal mass must be insulated from the outside. This could be a concrete floor that is insulated from the ground, or a large brick or rock feature inside the home. One form of this is called a **Trombe wall**. It is a dark-colored masonry or rock wall inside a home on which the sun shines during the day, collecting heat. During the evening this heat is gradually released into the house. If there were a day that was too warm, then a curtain could be drawn across the window so that the Trombe wall does not heat up. The wall could be only a few inches from the window, so that the interior of the house is not broken up by a large wall.

The temperature underground can be estimated by taking the average year-round temperature of your area and subtracting 10 degrees Fahrenheit. If this temperature is too cold, then using a thermal mass connected to the ground will not help your comfort—you will have to add a lot of heat to your house to overcome the cold from the ground and make it comfortable. If this temperature is too warm then you will be too hot during the summer and have to use a lot of air conditioning.

If you live in a climate that is hot and humid and it does

not sufficiently cool off at night, your only option may be refrigeration cooling—standard air conditioning. The resilient step is to invest in solar electric panels to power them. The good thing is that for much of the day, the greatest demand for cooling coincides with the greatest amount of sun for the panels, especially if the panels face toward the southwest. Therefore, even though refrigerated air conditioning uses a great deal of energy, a net zero or off-grid system is still feasible.

The most common method of air conditioning is refrigeration using an electric compressor. This compresses a special gas into a liquid. When the tube with this liquid enters the refrigerator or the air cooling chamber, it turns back into a gas, thus absorbing heat and cooling the house or refrigerator.

Absorption Cooling: An alternate way of refrigerating is by using a closed loop of water and lithium bromide. A heat source separates the two and boils the water in a near-vacuum environment. The principle was invented by Michael Faraday in 1824. The heat source can be anything—solar radiation, an electric heating element, propane, or any other combustible material. Recreational vehicles usually have refrigerators that work on this principle so that they can use propane to run it when not connected to the grid. Since the liquids and gasses involved move by convection, there are no pumps or other moving parts, except a fan to cool the coils in the case of an air conditioner. Therefore, refrigerators and air conditioners using this system usually last a long time. The only complication is that the refrigerator or air conditioner must be in a level position to work, which can sometimes be an issue in an RV, but not in a home system.

In some parts of the country, particularly in desert areas,

some people have house air conditioners that run on natural gas using this method. Therefore, it is theoretically possible to have not only a refrigerator but also a house air conditioning system powered by biogas from your own digester (see Chapter 2). But, as previously noted, heating or cooling a house involves a lot of energy, so your biogas system would have to be much larger than those designed to supply only a stove.

Savings from this step that can be invested: Residents of very cold or hot climates can save most or even all of their heating and cooling costs from this step, which can be substantial each month of the season when they are used. A passive system would require very little monitoring or repair, since there are no moving parts.

NEW DEVELOPMENTS TO WATCH FOR

- Monitor the U.S. Green Building Council website, with particular attention to their LEED (Leadership in Energy and Environmental Design) program: https://www.usgbc.org/.
- New insulation materials and techniques.
- Radiant paint or materials that cool a surface compared to the ambient air.
- Changes in building codes that allow or require passive heating and cooling building techniques in lieu of traditional heating or cooling systems that would not be needed and create added expense.

CHAPTER 4
FOOD

Whoever works his land will have plenty of bread,
but he who follows worthless pursuits lacks sense.
Solomon, Proverbs 12:11

My green thumb came only as a result
of the mistakes I made while learning to
see things from the plant's point of view.
H. Fred Ale

As the 2020 pandemic has shown, many people panic about having enough food if they are forced to stay home. What would you do if you could not go to a grocery store or get takeout food for one week? For two weeks? For a month?

At the beginning of the pandemic, stores were suddenly cleaned out of foods with a long shelf life such as pasta, beans, and canned foods. To the extent that you can provide your own food without going to a store, and without having a garage full of canned food, you will be more resilient. You can do this by **growing food** yourself, **hunting**, **trapping** and **fishing**, and **foraging** out in nature. The more that each family is able to do these things, the more resilient their community will be as a whole. When a disaster strikes, you will not contribute to the panic buying at the supermarket and will have extra to share with others when the need arises.

Everyone loves to see plants grow in their own garden and eat the results. They are tastier, fresher, and as organic as you would like them to be. It is also very educational to bring children into this process so they see the seeds sprout and grow, make flowers, and fruit. Retired folks can also participate in putting food on the table from a garden.

Hunting, trapping, and fishing are pastimes enjoyed by many people around the world as a hobby, but it is a useful hobby that increases resilience. There are some places around the world where this provides the majority of the food for the community, even now in the 21st century. Trapping is not as popular but can contribute to resilience in rural areas.

Another way to provide your own food is to forage for edible wild plants in your own region. Edible wild plants in North America include mustard greens and flowers, various berries, mushrooms, dandelions, clover, nasturtiums, stinging nettles, prickly pear cactus, bay leaves, cattails, watercress, fennel, and miner's lettuce (purslane). These are just a few of the more widespread examples. Each region of the continent has its own additions to this list. Many other leaves, seeds, fruits, and roots of wild plants can be eaten raw or cooked, used as a flavoring, or used as a tea infusion.

LEVEL 1: GARDEN IN A POT, TRY FISHING, FIND FOOD IN NATURE

Grow Your Own: For your first level of growing your own food, invest in a large pot and plant easy-to-grow vegetables and herbs on your balcony or deck. You can do this even if you live in an apartment, as long as your balcony or deck gets some sun.

For a no-expense way to go, cut the bottoms off of some 2-liter soda bottles, put a few small holes in the caps, turn them upside down, and suspend them using some bent clothes hangers, string or wire, or by putting nails in a horizontal board.

Parsley growing in a soda bottle, hanging on my fence by a nail

Green onions, tomatoes, basil, radishes, and spinach are particularly easy. For green onions, just buy some at the supermarket, and when you eat them, leave about 1 inch above the roots. Put the roots into a dish of water for a day or two, and then plant them in your pot roots down with just a little bit showing above the soil. They will provide you with fresh greens for years if your area does not have a hard frost. If they are in a pot, bring them inside when frosts begin and continue to enjoy them. Just cut off and eat the oldest leaf every week or so, and when they try to make a seed pod, cut it off. Spinach can be used the entire season—just pick the oldest leaves, and let the rest continue to grow. Tomatoes require a very sunny location to produce a bumper crop but can do well with moderate sun. Radishes are the fastest to mature.

You could fill your pot with dirt from your yard, or anywhere, but try to find soil with a good amount of organic matter in it already. If you have the money and want to be sure about the quality of your soil, use potting mix from your local hardware store or nursery. This is different from "planting mix" in that potting mix includes some vermiculite, a white porous mineral that soaks up water and gradually releases it to the plants. This is useful because pots tend to dry out much faster than in-ground gardens.

If you often travel on weekends or for a week or two, your pots will dry out, unless you get a friend to water them for you. But this problem can be taken care of if you use a "wicking" container. This has no hole at the bottom, but instead, a layer of rocks or sand. It is filled with water up to a certain level controlled by an overflow pipe or hole in the side of the container. The plant roots will go down to the level of the water and drink what they need. You put a plastic pipe in the corner of the container through which you add water. Such a container can go weeks without adding water, even in a dry climate. You can find detailed instructions on the internet.

Try Fishing: The first level of fishing is not too difficult. Find a local friend who knows how to fish in your region. Go out with him or her to fish once, and see how you like it. If you enjoy it, let them help you invest in an appropriate rod and reel, a few hooks, lures, bobbers, and sinkers, and perhaps some bait. All of these things would have to be appropriate for your local type and size of fish. A fly fishing rod and reel is completely different from a spin caster, and these are both different from a rig for large ocean fish. You will also need a fishing license in most cases, unless all your fishing will be on private property, or in the ocean from a pier. Then go together to your local lake, river, or ocean and go for it.

Forage in Nature: To begin to forage food in your area, first look online or in your local library for a list of local edible wild plants. Then consult a local person who is experienced in foraging. Go out with them and have them show you what some of the local edibles look like in their natural environment. Do not taste any wild food unless you are sure you can identify it, because some poisonous plants look very similar to edible ones.

To begin, pick one that is very easy to identify and easy to use, such as wild mustard. It is easily recognized by its bright yellow flowers and grows to between 3 and 6 feet high in the summer. The leaves can be eaten raw, but they are very much like spinach when boiled or steamed for just a minute or two. The flowers are great as a garnish on a salad either raw or soaked in vinegar for a few days. The roots can also be eaten, but are usually quite tough, so I stick to the leaves and flowers.

Stinging nettles are also easy to recognize by their "hairy" leaves and stems. Bring some gloves and a bag on a hike and collect some. If you boil the leaves for 30 seconds, they will no longer sting you and are tasty and very nutritious.

Fiddlehead ferns are common throughout North America and can be boiled and eaten when they are coming up in the spring and early summer.

All parts of the dandelion plant are also edible raw or cooked, and they are very easy to identify. New leaves can be used in a salad. Some say that the flowers are particularly nutritious.

The leaves, vine tips, flowers and roots of kudzu vines are edible, but the vines themselves are not.[1] This is an invasive species in southeastern states, so the more you eat, the better! Likewise, watercress is invasive, and also very nutritious. Narrow-leaved cattails can also be eaten, and will help to eliminate an invader.

For all these greens, use plants that are away from roadways, not likely to have been soiled by passing dogs or sprayed by a nearby homeowner. Don't just pull weeds—eat them!

Savings from this step that can be invested: Modest savings can be attained with this step in the purchase of fresh greens. As for my own family, we have not purchased green onions or kale for several years, and we use them often.

LEVEL 2: SMALL RAISED BED GARDEN, COMPOSTING, SERIOUS FISHING, FURTHER FORAGING

Small Garden: Even a small raised-bed garden can grow a lot of food. Find some lumber and create a rectangle 2 or 3 feet wide by 6 or 8 feet long, and 2 or 3 feet high. If you have gophers or other underground rodents in your neighborhood, line the bottom with chicken wire before you fill it with soil. If you have deer, raccoons, or opossums in your area that can access your yard, then you may need to make a wire covering over the top as well.

If you live in an area subject to drought or you will be

---

1. Did You Know You Can Eat Kudzu? | The Kitchn

gone for a week or so from time to time and cannot monitor your garden's need for water, then a **self-wicking raised bed** garden is the way to go. Construct a raised bed frame as above, but make it at least 3 or 4 feet high. Line the entire frame on the inside with a thick plastic, so as to create something like a bathtub. At the bottom, put in 1 foot of rocks, being careful not to puncture the plastic. At the 1 foot level, drill a hole in the side of the frame and insert a piece of pipe. This is your overflow outlet. Cover the rocks and the overflow pipe with a layer of landscape fabric that is water permeable. In one corner put a vertical pipe that reaches below the landscape fabric—this is your fill pipe. Then fill the rest of the frame with good garden soil and plant your crop. With a hose, fill the bottom of your self-wicking garden with water until it starts to come out of the overflow tube. The water in this bottom later will wick up through the soil, keeping it moist as needed, while the top inch or so remains dry. See the videos in the appendix for more details. This can also be done with any kind of pot, as long as you can make a hole in the side for overflow.

If you have only a small space to work with, there are several things you can do. For my own "pandemic garden" I made a three-tier raised-bed garden out of spare lumber and placed it on the south side of our house. The bottom tier is about 3 feet wide and sits on the ground.

The second tier is 3 feet above the first and recessed so that the sun can shine on the bottom tier. The third tier is 2.5 feet above the second, and recessed from the second, so it is only about 8 inches wide. This way, I doubled my garden space in a very narrow south-facing side yard. On the bottom level are several kale plants and a potato. In the middle, are spinach (left rear), green onions, kale, and a flower. The top level was fallow at the time of the photo.

Another strategy is to make a garden in bottles on a south-facing wall that gets plenty of sun. Make or purchase a lattice of wood about 6 feet high. On this lattice, hang 2-liter soda bottle planters, using wire or string. In this way, you can cover the entire lattice with plants.

If you live in an apartment with no balcony, you may be able to grow some plants indoors if there is a window that faces the sun. Or see if your neighborhood has a community garden with plots where you can grow something. If there isn't one, then get together with some others in your neighborhood and see if you can get one started. As an alternative, you could be a "guerrilla gardener"—scatter some seeds in a public area and see what happens.

In some cases, you do not even have to buy seeds. Some vegetables can be grown from kitchen scraps, such as anything in the onion family (green, yellow, or red onions; leeks; garlic), potatoes (all types), ginger, celery, fennel, cabbage, beet greens, and many types of herbs. Some grocery stores now sell lettuce with the roots intact. You can eat most of it, plant the inner part with the roots and a few of the smaller leaves, and then keep eating it all season. See Appendix 2 under Chapter 4 for a link to a video about how to plant using scraps.

Zucchini, tomatoes, and cabbage are not difficult to grow. For example, one summer I harvested almost 55 pounds of zucchini from only four plants. I let the zucchini grow to between 1 and 4 pounds each rather than picking them when they are very young, like the ones in the supermarket. The largest ones we used to make stuffed zucchini—yum! A disadvantage is that the seeds in the center portion are no longer edible. Also, if the zucchini get to be about 6 to

8 pounds, the skin is too tough to eat, even if baked, similar to a butternut squash. My record is an 8-pound zucchini.

Easy-to-grow, versatile, productive, healthy, and tasty vegetables include lettuce, carrots, cabbage, beets, onions, cucumbers, peas, beans, tomatoes, and potatoes. As a strategy for saving money during normal times, I would concentrate on the crops that are the most expensive to buy in the store or are much better tasting when home-grown. These would include tomatoes, red and green onions, peas, and beans. I would also include kale, bok choy, and other less popular but tasty and nutritious greens. But your strategy in a survival situation might change to grow those crops that would provide the most calories and nutrients: potatoes, cabbage, beans, and squash.

A strategy for those with some **space but little time** to devote to gardening is to plant **perennial foods**—those that do not need to be planted again year after year. These plants either keep growing from year to year, or regrow from the ground up by themselves each spring. These include fruit trees and berry bushes, grapes, and vegetables such as green onions, chives, garlic, artichokes, Babington's leek, Egyptian walking onion, capers, asparagus, rhubarb, sorrel, lovage, watercress, radicchio, and some varieties of kale, cauliflower, and broccoli. Perennial tubers include sunchokes, potatoes, horseradish, and oka (New Zealand yam). Perennial herbs include rosemary, horseradish (try the leaves!), and lavender. Perennial flowers such as nasturtiums and calendula are edible, as well as ground cover like purslane.

If your garden area is shaded by trees or buildings, do not despair. Many food plants actually do better in **partial shade**, defined as only three to five hours of sun per day. These include many leafy greens, such as lettuce, spinach, cilantro, kale, parsley, basil, and chard. Radishes will also do fine, though they will take a little longer to mature. Green onions and chives will also do OK. Bush beans, sweet potatoes, and cherry tomatoes will grow, but the harvest will be slightly smaller. Mint will grow in total shade, and is actually harmed by strong sunlight. But never try to grow corn, large tomatoes, potatoes, chilies, cucumbers, or okra in even partial shade—they like full sun. In some cases, you can position a large piece of reflective material in such a way that your shaded garden area receives reflected sunlight.

One technique for maximum yield in a small space is "Three Sisters Planting." Native Americans would grow corn, squash, and pole beans on small mounds. Planting the corn first, the beans would climb up the corn stalks, and the squash plants would cover the ground around them, keeping it more moist. Any variety of these three crops works in this way. All bean varieties work to put nitrogen into the soil, which the other two crops need to thrive and are a good source of protein.

Example #1: How *dachas* saved people in the former Soviet Union in the '90s.

A *dacha* is a plot of land outside of the city for city-dwellers to "get away" for the weekend. It is similar to an "allotment" in the U.K., or a "Garten" (garden) in Germany, but larger. In practice, most are used to grow vegetables and fruit and often have a small shelter where the owner can spend the night during summer weekends. Russian housing consists of about 30% single-family houses and 70% apartments (condos). The population of Russia in 1990 was 150 million, of which 105 million lived in apartments. If there were an average of three people in each apartment, then there were probably about 35 million apartments. At that time there were 60 million dachas in Russia. Therefore, most apartment dwellers in Russia had access to a dacha. If they did not have one themselves, then a close friend or relative had one.

The standard dacha consists of 6 *sotok,* meaning 600 square meters, which is about 0.14 acre (about 1/7), or 6,458 square feet. The most common foods planted at dachas are potatoes, onions, tomatoes, cucumbers, carrots, cabbages, and other vegetables; berries; and fruit, depending on latitude and altitude. Flowers are also popular. Potatoes and cabbage are excellent survival foods. All these foods are easily stored for the winter in cellars (potatoes, cabbage, onions, carrots, beets, apples) or they are canned (tomatoes, cucumbers, berries, and other fruit).

When the Soviet Union collapsed at the end of 1991, the economy collapsed with it. Unemployment quickly went up to over 50% in many places. Even those still employed were paid very little, or their employers had no money to pay them. The only reason why huge numbers did not starve to death was that they could grow their own food at their dacha, and store it for winter in a cellar at the dacha or in the basement of their apartment building, or they could can or dehydrate it. If they had a surplus, they would sell it at their neighborhood bazaar. They were resilient!

Example #2: Victory gardens of WWII. Victory gardens helped win World War II because they allowed the U.S. government to divert scarce tin supplies from making cans to military use. They also promoted healthier eating habits, since fresh, home-grown vegetables supplied 40 percent of the produce grown in the United States by 1944. People planted 20 million victory gardens across the United States during the war. They sprang up on school grounds, in vacant city lots, in apartment window boxes, and on rooftops.

Newspapers printed gardening advice, and competitions were held. We were resilient!

Example #3: Pandemic gardening in 2020. As soon as the COVID-19 pandemic hit, more people started gardening. Seed suppliers were completely cleaned out in the early days of lockdown. Many of those customers were first-time growers. There were two drivers of this trend: empty grocery store shelves in the early part of the pandemic, and people having to stay home and find something useful to do. Even though it was not for the most part the vegetable aisles of stores that were empty, just the sight of paper goods being out of stock made people think that anything could be next. Growing their own food also gave many people a sense of purpose and contributing to society in a small way. It helped our resilience, both physically and psychologically.

Example #4: Vietnamese immigrants have been through many hard times and have therefore learned how to be resilient. Wherever they live, they plant gardens "wall to wall," including even the front yards of urban homes. Thus, they provide much of their own food. This proved very wise during the COVID-19 pandemic.

Example #5: A couple in Pasadena, California produce 6,000 pounds of food in their yard of 1/10 of an acre using intensive techniques.[2]

. . .

2. Family reveals how they grow 6,000 pounds of food a year on just 1/10 of an acre: 'Farming is full of ups and downs' (msn.com)

Composting: Make your own compost from kitchen scraps and fallen leaves. Just leave out bones or other items that do not decompose, and don't use eucalyptus leaves or too many pine needles that contain oils or tannins that are not helpful.

The compost bins that are easiest to use easily rotate and have two sections—see the photo of my own unit. Fill one section and then start on the second. Rotate the bins at least twice every time you add fresh material. When the second section is full, then the first section should be ready to be emptied into your garden. The advantage of this type is the ease of mixing. The disadvantage is that it is difficult to keep the compost damp, because necessary moisture leaks out the bottom and evaporates from all sides, leaving you with dry clumps. Keep the compost bin in a warm, sunny location. The decomposition process creates some heat of its own, but the warmer it is, the faster the process goes.

Irrigation: If you live in a dry climate, consider how you will water your garden. A self-wicking raised bed is one way. Another water-saving method would be drip irrigation or soaker hoses. Overhead sprinklers would use the most water.

Serious Fishing: For second-level fishing, you can think about investing in a boat, if that would be advantageous for the type of fishing in your area. The type and size of boat will depend on the body of water you are fishing in and how far you must travel to the fishing grounds. It might be just a rowboat or canoe. For river fishing, you might just need waders. If you are near the ocean and like swimming, you could try spearfishing, for which you would need a wet suit, fins, mask and snorkel, a speargun, and a special bag for the fish you catch, as well as a fishing license. If spearfishing is really your thing, you could learn how to scuba dive and invest in scuba gear, although it is sufficient in many locations to spearfish with only a mask and snorkel.

Simple Hunting Without Guns: There are some animals that do not require a gun to hunt, such as bullfrogs. Use a "frog gig" to catch them for eating—a long pole with three to five barbed prongs. Most places have a season for them and require a hunting license, but in Utah, since they are an invasive species, the season is always open. Frog legs taste like chicken.

Further Foraging: For second-level foraging, you must first invest some time in research. The Native Americans lived on the plants and animals native to your region. Therefore, go to your local museum that shows how they lived, what they ate, and how they gathered, prepared, and stored it. You might also find this information in your local library, or a bookstore which stocks locally-written books. Also invest in a physical book (not an electronic one, unless you can take your tablet out in the field) of wild food in your region.

Then choose two or three more wild foods that you would like to target. Go out with someone in the know about them, collect some, and try them. At this level, you could also try some wild foods that are more difficult or time-consuming to prepare.

. . .

Example: Acorns. In California, the Native Americans ate acorn meal as a staple food. Collect some acorns in the fall —the bigger the better. Different oak species produce different-sized acorns—I have found that white oaks generally produce the largest. The laborious part is shelling them. Once that is done, boil them for about 10 to 15 minutes and throw away the water, which has become very dark with bitter tannin. Lay the nuts out in the sun to dry, but not so long that they become hard. Put the semi-dry nuts into a food processor and pulverize them into a rough powder. The Native Americans did this step by hand with a stone mortar and pestle. This acorn flour can be used to make bread or muffins in a 40/60 or 50/50 mixture with wheat flour so that the gluten in the wheat binds it together. It gives the food a delicious nutty taste, and it is nutritious as well. You can store the acorn flour in the refrigerator for a week or so. If you wish to store it longer, you must put it in the freezer. This is because the flour is not totally dry, making it a target for mold.

Savings from this step that can be invested: A significant amount of a family's grocery budget can be saved by this level, particularly in the summer.

LEVEL 3: ADVANCED GARDENING, HUNTING, FINER POINTS OF FORAGING

Advanced Gardening: At this level, you can **harvest your own seeds for next year**. You must use non-hybrid seeds to start on this. Seeds from the fruit of plants from hybrid seeds will not always sprout.

At this level, you can also **use gray water** for your garden if you are in a drought-prone area. (See Chapter 6: Water.) You will expand the area devoted to planting, and the variety of things that you plant. Your garden will supply most of your fresh vegetables during the summer and into the autumn.

You will also go into **serious composting**, because your larger garden will need nutrients, and you want to avoid the need to buy large quantities of fertilizer. For this, you will need compost piles, rather than a small plastic mixer. To create your compost pile, try to use 60% "browns" and 40% "greens." Browns are organic material that has been dead for a while and are brown in color—wood chips, sawdust, straw, dry leaves and twigs, etc. Greens include fresh tree trimmings, food scraps and trimmings from the kitchen, grass cuttings, and also animal droppings, especially from herbivores like horses, cows, goats, rabbits, or poultry. About a quarter of your greens should be from this source if possible. Mix the items thoroughly, and make the whole pile moist but not dripping wet. In about a day, if you have done it right, the pile will start to get hot—even up to 160 degrees F. This heat will kill all the weed seeds so the resulting compost will not spread weeds or other plants you don't want into your garden.

At this level, you should also learn about **fertilizer**. All plants need three elements to thrive: nitrogen (N), phosphorus (P, from phosphates), and potassium (symbol K, derived from potash). Different plants require differing shares of these elements, and commercial fertilizers are labeled with numbers indicating the relative shares. First, find out what your crops need, and then test your soil (after adding your compost) to see what is already there. If you already have enough of a certain element, then don't add any more—it could actually hurt the plants.

As a side benefit, you can **harvest heat** from the compost pile by putting some plastic water tubing through it and pumping the water in a loop to a place where you need heat, such as your greenhouse in the winter, or perhaps a shop building. The larger the pile, the longer it will stay hot.

Fishing with a Side Benefit: There are some fish that have been introduced from overseas that have become a nuisance because they have no local natural enemies and crowd out the environment for native fish. Asian carp are one such fish, but there are others. Naturalists encourage people to take as many of such fish as possible, compared to native species, for which there may be limits on the number you can catch. Carp are a very bony fish, which is why some people do not like them, but they are good tasting, and very popular in Asia for eating. Learn how to catch and prepare them, and help the environment at the same time. Likewise, red swamp crayfish are also invasive, so let's eat as many as possible!

Hunting with guns starts here at Level 3. This is because you must invest in a rifle (for mammals) or a shotgun (for birds), a hunting safety course, a general hunting license from your state, special tags for certain larger animals, and ammunition. Then you must do some target practice to get used to your weapon and gain some accuracy. So you are talking about a significant investment of both money and time. If you are hunting smaller animals, it is possible that one of the new powerful air rifles could be used, which would make your ammunition much cheaper. Some have even hunted wild pigs with air rifles. A bonus is that the quietness of shots with this weapon means that shooting one animal does not frighten away the rest of the herd, and you can bag several of them at once.

For many animals, there is a particular **hunting season**,

often in the fall. Generally, you would then have to travel (more expense) to an area where the animals you are hunting are prevalent. If you or a good friend live outside of an incorporated city and have a large piece of land, it is possible that you can safely hunt certain animals on private property.

In Texas, wild hogs are such a nuisance that you are allowed to hunt them without even a license at any time of the year and any time of the day or night. It was recently reported that there are 6 million feral hogs in 35 states and also in many parts of Canada. These are not native to North America, so even hunting them to extinction would be a good thing.

Likewise, invasive green iguanas are running rampant in Florida, destroying habitat and canal banks. They are supposed to taste like rabbit or dark chicken meat, and they can be hunted with high powered air rifles. For those into more exotic hunting, pythons have also invaded Florida.

Nutria are invasive in Louisiana and nearby Southern states, and destroy habitat. They also taste like rabbit, and can be hunted anytime. The State of Louisiana will pay $6 for each nutria tail that is turned in.

There may be other **nuisance animals** that can be hunted in your state.

Find a friend who is already a hunter and learn the particulars about hunting in your region. In some parts of North America like Alaska, hunting and fishing is a way of life, and this is how they obtain a good part of their diet. But people in many areas supplement their diet with hunted food. Hunting also includes trapping with snares or traps.

Finer Points of Foraging: Level 3 foraging involves identifying more difficult plants such as **mushrooms**. These require special care, because many varieties in North

America are very poisonous, and they look very similar to edible European and Asian varieties. Every few years some immigrants from Asia get very sick or even die from eating poisonous mushrooms by mistake.

You could also get even more adventuresome and **include small animals** in your foraging, including garden snails, acorn grubs and other grubs, mole crabs, and various insects such as wood shrimp (pill bugs). People in other parts of the world eat these as a regular part of their diet. At the right locations and time of year, **mollusks** can be harvested from the ocean shore, such as mussels, limpets or clams. In general, it is safe to eat shellfish from the tidal zone only during cold months, when the bacteria counts are low. Be sure to get a fishing license, and consult local people who know about this.

While you are at the shore, don't forget about **seaweed**. All types are edible, although some types are more appetizing than others. The Welsh eat *laverbread*, and Russians eat *morskaya kapusta* (literally, sea cabbage)—both of them a type of seaweed. It is a staple of Korean salads and in Japanese cuisine. Sushi is often wrapped in it. Find a local person who can guide you as to how, when, and what kind to harvest, and how to prepare and eat it. Check if you will need a fishing license, which areas may be off limits to harvesting such as parks, and if there is a limit on your daily harvest. If you harvest it responsibly, there will continue to be an abundance of it for the eating.

Savings from this step that can be invested: A large part of a family's grocery budget can be saved with a large garden of this type, and your health will also benefit, thus saving doctor bills in the long run.

LEVEL 4: SELF-SUFFICIENCY IN FRUIT AND VEGETABLES

Ultimately, given enough space and time, you can become completely self-sufficient in fruits and vegetables. This is possible if you have about a half to a whole acre for each person in the household, depending on your climate zone and the fertility of your soil. For a family of four, three estimates of the area needed ranged between 1.76 and 2 acres. In places like Southern California and Arizona, south Texas, the Gulf Coast, and Florida, you can grow fruits and vegetables all year, so the amount of land could be less. In areas such as Montana, Idaho, and Colorado, it might be quite a bit larger. If you are a vegan, you would then be totally self-sufficient in food, with the exception of oils and some special soy or nut products.

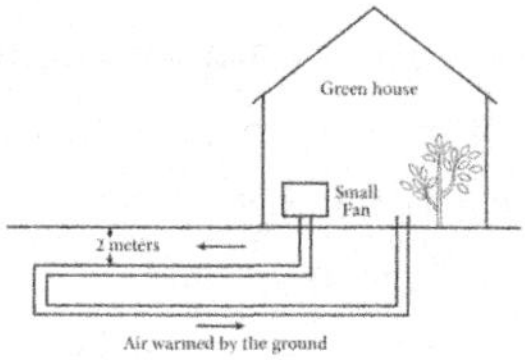

You can grow food year-round farther north as well if you invest in **cold frames** or **greenhouses**. A cold frame is a raised bed garden with a glass or plastic cover—you do not walk into it, as you would a greenhouse, but rather tend it from the sides. If you go even farther north, you can still use a greenhouse in the winter by sinking it several feet into the ground, insulating the north side, and covering the entire structure with insulation every evening. You can also use low-level geothermal heat by burying long tubes at least 6 feet (2 meters) underground with a small fan to circulate air from these tubes into the greenhouse—see diagram.[3]

3. Diagram by arafat_creative through fiverr.com

Northern climate greenhouses: One person in Nebraska grows oranges in such a greenhouse, using no outside energy.[4] (Orange trees are damaged by frost, can be killed by a frost below 25 degrees F, and Nebraska can be below zero in the winter.) Another person grows vegetables in the winter at 52 degrees latitude, north of Calgary, Alberta, without any heating unit. It gets down to 40 degrees below zero there. So, it is possible to grow your food year-round almost anywhere, although in northern latitudes it will require more investment. See Appendix 2, Chapter 4 about links to the Central Alberta gardener and other people who have greenhouses in cold climates.

Other ways to **keep a greenhouse warm without outside energy** include a large compost heap, capturing solar energy in large black water-filled barrels (or other thermal mass), and using the body heat of large animals such as cows, sheep, or goats in an adjacent barn. A well-mixed and moist compost heap will get up to 160 degrees, and one that is 6 to 8 feet in diameter and 4 feet high will generate heat for many months. The bonus is that when it is finished creating heat for you, it is ready to be fertilizer for your garden.

In high latitudes the outdoor growing season is rather short, so many people start their vegetable seedlings indoors under **grow lights**. If you buy these, shop carefully. Some suppliers advertise 45-watt LED, but when you look down in the specifications, the light actually uses only 13 watts—the 45 refers to the equivalent power of a CFL or incandescent light. You can buy premium "full spectrum" lights, but regular LED lights will work just as well if you look for "daylight" bulbs as opposed to "soft white" types. If you search for "grow lights" you will buy the same basic light

---

4. https://www.youtube.com/watch?v=ZD_3_gsgsnk&t=664s

but pay several times more money. Be aware that you must install the lights very close to the growing plants, but not so close that the plants will become burned by the intensity. So as the plants grow, you must adjust your lights upward and the space in your racks for seedlings must accommodate this. Use LED rather than fluorescent shop lights.[5] Florescent lights use more power, and create a lot of heat—too much as spring advances.

It would not be efficient in most cases to grow, harvest, and process wheat, rice, or other grains for just one family. So **for carbohydrates,** you could grow potatoes, yams, sweet potatoes, and similar root crops. Corn can also easily be grown for one family, and if you grew Aztec-style corn, it can be hung up to dry and kept that way for many months until you ground it for cornmeal.

Creating a **food forest** is one way to grow a variety of food in a relatively small space. This means an area where there are many levels or layers of plants, one above the other. At the top layer are fruit or nut trees. Below them would be bushes, such as various kinds of berries. Among and below the berries could be root or leafy vegetables. Winding through all of them would be vines such as grapes or passion fruit. The result looks like a jungle, but all the plants and fruit are edible, and it is a very efficient use of space. A food forest is self-mulching, and since it includes many varieties of plants, it will feed you for much of the year—even all year in lower latitudes.

Savings from this step that can be invested: Your entire food budget except for meat and some specialty items could be saved by this step.

5. https://www.youtube.com/watch?v=dsya6ySIy-Q

LEVEL 5: SELF-SUFFICIENCY IN ALL FOOD

Given enough land, and if you make it a nearly full-time occupation, you can become self-sufficient in all your food needs, including eggs, dairy, and meat. Many people raise **chickens, ducks, geese, turkeys or quail** (check with your city about what's allowed, if you live in an urban area) or **rabbits**. All of them breed very quickly and can live in small spaces. In some places, you are allowed to have chickens but not roosters because of the noise. Other places limit the number of any one animal. A pond or container with **fish** such as tilapia could also supply protein and would also not take much space. If you live in a rural area and have a large property, you could think about cattle, sheep, goats, pigs or other large animals. One advantage of keeping animals is that their dung makes excellent fertilizer for your crops.

Remember that to be completely self-sufficient, you would have to raise enough **feed for these animals** as well. Chickens eat sunflower seeds, which are easy to grow but hard to harvest and shell for human consumption. For chickens, just cut off the large sunflower head and throw it in their enclosure, and they are good to go. Since the original habitat of chickens was the jungles of Southeast Asia, the more you keep them in a place resembling that condition, the easier and cheaper they will be to keep. All fowl eat bugs and thus help to protect your vegetables. Bugs also give them good protein.

You would also be advised to procure one or more large guard dogs to keep predators away from your animals. Dogs also keep deer away from your fruit trees and vegetables. But even with dogs, coyotes and foxes in the neighborhood will eventually find your birds and eat them. In such areas, you can make a movable chicken house with wheels on one end. When the chickens finish eating the bugs and vegetation in one area, move the whole house to another.

For an even further step, you could **grow your own fiber**: wool, flax, hemp, sisal, etc. This would take even more space, and processing the fiber would require a lot of effort.

If you have or develop a self-sufficient farm, you **may need a tractor**. In that case, consider investing in an electric one. You would not have the "range" issues that people have with electric cars, because you would not be driving it very far from your house. You would always be able to fuel it at home, it would not require as much maintenance, and it would not be noisy or polluting. Several companies are now making small electric tractors.[6]

Ultimate level: Permaculture This is a system of growing crops and animal husbandry in which the waste of one crop is the fertilizer for another, and the entire operation makes the land richer and more productive over time, rather than less. It is "a conscious design of agriculturally productive ecosystems that have the diversity, stability and resilience of natural ecosystems."[7]

Example: Emma Naluyima of Uganda, as seen on a Ted Talk on YouTube—see Appendix 2 for a link. Emma has only 1 acre of originally red-colored soil, indicating poor soil with a lack of organic matter. She practices what she calls "integrated farming."

---

6. https://solectrac.com/Case tractor: https://www.youtube.com/watch?v=u-i08DJNYTY

7. https://www.tenthacrefarm.com/what-is-permaculture/, quoting Bill Mollison, co-founder and father of the movement.

In one quarter of the area, she keeps pigs. The pig dung is put in the sun in a heap where flies lay their eggs in it. The eggs turn into maggots in only a few days. The maggots are strained out and given to her chickens and fish, which thrive on the protein. The remaining dung is seeded with earthworms, which turn it into quality fertilizer.

Another quarter of her property has milk cows. Their dung is fed into a biomass digester, which turns the dung into methane for cooking. The liquid from the digester is used as fertilizer, as is the urine from the cows.

Another quarter is planted with plantains, the staple food of the region. The final quarter has fish farming in ponds and aquaponic containers. Dung from the fish becomes fertilizer for the aquaponic tomatoes, and also for the plants that are fodder for the pigs and cows.

She sells pork, eggs, milk, plantains, catfish, tilapia, and tomatoes in her local market, and with the proceeds, she supports her family and the operation of a school. All of this on 1 acre with initially poor soil! She is certainly an example of resilience.

Extra bonus #1: The food is fresher, tastier, and organic. Unless you live in California, most of the vegetables in a typical supermarket come from hundreds or even thousands of miles away and are picked when still green (unripe). This is particularly the case with tomatoes, which are often therefore tasteless. In addition, unless you pay a premium for organically grown produce, they have been treated with pesticides. Food from your own garden is picked the same day you eat it and will be free of contamination if you choose.

. . .

Extra bonus #2: You can grow things not carried in your local supermarket, such as Asian fruits and vegetables. We grow sunchokes (also known as Jerusalem artichokes), which are very easy to grow, come up year after year by themselves, and are hard to find in stores.

These ideas are only a beginning, and you would need to do research as to what can most easily be grown in your area, given your temperatures, precipitation, and soils. However, you can use greenhouses to help with temperatures, irrigate to supplement precipitation, and add compost to improve your soil. You can even use grow lights to supplement the lack of sunshine in the winter at high latitudes, although that could entail a lot of energy.

Savings from this step that can be invested: Your entire food budget for the year is covered by this step.

NEW DEVELOPMENTS TO WATCH FOR

- New organic ways to deter or get rid of pests that eat your crops.
- New places to source heirloom, non-hybrid seeds, and plants.
- New gardening, fishing, hunting, or foraging clubs in your area.

CHAPTER 5
COOKING AND PRESERVING FOOD

Principles have no real force
except when one is well fed.
Mark Twain

I've known what it is to be hungry,
but I always went right to a restaurant.
Ring Lardner (1885-1933)

I don't even butter my bread.
I consider that cooking.
Katherine Cebrian

When the Covid-19 pandemic started, our daughter told us that there were many people she knew in her urban area who had been eating in restaurants or buying takeout food from restaurants and grocery stores for nearly all their meals. They went into panic mode when these options were closed or restricted. Some of them had no idea how to cook a meal from raw ingredients or even canned ingredients, and had no supply of those ingredients at home. They were not resilient in terms of cooking and preserving food.

In addition to being useful during an emergency, **cooking from scratch** saves a lot of money, compared with buying the same foods ready-made from the supermarket, and certainly compared to eating takeout food from restaurants. A small investment of time to cook this way can save a significant amount of money during normal times. In addition, if you have a financial setback, you are more resilient because you are already prepared to economize. And if supply chain issues prevent you from obtaining any particular canned or processed food, you are ready to make it yourself, or use a substitute. For example, one family in the Midwest says that they save $2,000 per year by preparing and preserving their own food. They are also more resilient, having four months' worth of food at home.[1]

Preserving food yourself takes time, but it is an investment that saves money. You can buy fruit and vegetables when they are cheap (or even free!), and then eat them later in a season when they are expensive. Ways of preserving food include:

- **Freezing**—easy, but you may need to invest in a large or separate freezer for large quantities
- **Drying**—invest in a dehydrator (much cheaper than a large freezer) and some time
- **Canning**—invest in canning jars, and some time
- **Pickling**—includes more than just cucumbers
- **Cellar storage**—for root crops, cabbage, some kinds of fruit, cheeses, and preserved meats.

1. 'I'm a mass prepper saving thousands a year - here's how I stock up for FOUR months' (msn.com)

- **Evaporation cooler**—simple to construct
- **Ice house**—for colder climates
- **Fermenting**—beer, wine, and other less well-known products

As you progress through the levels, pass on what you have learned to someone else in your household (your children, certainly) or community. By doing this you will increase the resilience of your community as a whole and also solidify the knowledge in your own life.

Most of these steps do not involve buying things that have parts made overseas, so these steps cannot be disrupted by supply chain problems.

LEVEL 1: COOK FOR YOURSELF EASILY PREPARED, HIGH-COST FOODS, PRESERVE BY FREEZING, DRYING, COOLERS, AND WINTER TEMPERATURES

Cooking: Foods that are easy to prepare but cost a lot to buy include granola, soup, salad dressing, and bread. **Granola** is simply oats, nuts or seeds, perhaps some spices, and some oil, baked in the oven. If you like dried fruit in your granola, you would add that after it is cooked. The ingredients cost approximately $2.15 to $3.15 per pound to make yourself, depending on how many and what kind of nuts you put in, but it costs between $4.32 and $5.00 per pound to buy in the supermarket. The important figures here are not the absolute numbers, which can change from week to week and store to store, but the relative costs of the ingredients compared to store-bought, which will be about the same in any case. You can find many recipes online, but a simple recipe is in Appendix 1.

A **vinaigrette salad dressing** is simply vinegar, water,

oil, and some spices. It is easy to make it yourself in a cruet that is handily marked with levels for the proper amounts of vinegar, water, and oil. It costs about 42 cents per cup to mix it yourself, but about 99 cents per cup to buy it in the supermarket. Supermarket varieties typically have about 240 mg of salt in 2 tablespoons, and 2 grams of sugar, which you may not want. You may want to use wine vinegar and olive oil, which would increase your homemade price to $1.27 per cup, but a premium vinaigrette from the store will be still higher. A recipe for a vinaigrette is included in Appendix 1. Other homemade salad dressing recipes are also available on the internet.

Making your own bread is a process, but can be greatly simplified by investing in a bread machine. Put the ingredients in the container, press the button, and in a little over two hours you have a hot fresh loaf. The ingredients cost only 74 cents for a 1-pound loaf of basic whole wheat, but it will cost you at least $1 in the store for the cheapest variety. A recipe is included in Appendix 1.

Soups are also easy to make yourself and cost much more to buy. The ingredients for chicken noodle soup cost only about 30 cents per cup, but a typical can of the same soup from the supermarket will be twice as much and has about 890 mg of sodium. Soups in general have the highest amount of sodium of any prepared food from the supermarket, except sauces. They generally add an excessive amount of salt to these products to give them flavor in lieu of adding herbs and spices, which would slightly increase the cost. Instead, save the bones from a chicken or turkey you have eaten and make a large pot of soup, which will feed you for many meals. Even if you buy low-salt varieties of soup at the store, which are often more expensive, they still have unhealthy levels of salt, which you can reduce or eliminate if you make it yourself.

Spaghetti sauce is simply tomatoes (or canned tomato sauce), vegetables, meat or tofu, and spices. Starting with canned tomato sauce, I have calculated that spaghetti sauce costs about 71 cents per pound with 260 mg of salt. Buying ready-made spaghetti sauce costs about $1.79 per pound, and has 450-480 mg of salt per half cup, which is not good for you.

Sauerkraut and kimchi are also foods that are simple and inexpensive to make but often more expensive to buy. The only equipment you need is a tall jar and a round potato masher. Cabbage costs from 75 cents to $1.29 per pound to buy, but canned sauerkraut from the store costs between 75 cents (at a dollar store) and $1.64 per pound. Kimchi is simply coarse sauerkraut with the addition of red pepper flakes.

The best part is that by making these foods yourself, you can make them exactly how you like them. If you like fruit in your granola, you can put exactly the kind you want. If you like nuts in your bread, you can add them. If you are trying to cut down on carbs, you can make your bread with bean or nut flour. You can make your kimchi as hot or as mild as you like. With all of these foods, you can also avoid an overload of salt and sugar, thus preserving your long-term health (see Chapter 8: Health). If you try to buy specialty items like these in the supermarket, you will pay a premium. For example, I have calculated that low carbohydrate bread costs about $5 to $7 per loaf to buy, but only $4 to $5 to make yourself.

Preserving: The easiest way to preserve food is to **freeze** it. Invest in some freezer-quality zip-top bags. Buy berries or other fruit or vegetables in season. Put them on a cookie sheet or large plate so that they are not touching each other and freeze. Then put them in the bags. If you put them in the bags first and then freeze, they will all freeze to each other, and it will be impossible to get them apart to use just a few of them. If you freeze many things, it can help to obtain vacuum sealing machine. This protects food from freezer burn, and helps you to fit more food into your freezer. It is also good for dried food, because excluding most of the oxygen in a bag will extend the shelf life.

Dehydrating is also easy. A dehydrator costs about $70 or so, and will dry several pounds of fruit or vegetables at a time—see photo of Make sure that you get a dehydrator that has a fan. The smaller and thinner the food items are, the faster the drying time will be, but generally it will take about six to eight hours. The time also depends on the humidity of your air. The advantages are that the food will shrink, so more can fit into zip-top bags for storage. It also will not need to be refrigerated or frozen. A third advantage is that dehydrated foods are great for taking on hikes or backpacking because they are very lightweight. If you puree the food before drying, you can make "fruit leather." This is an excellent way to deal with a surplus of backyard fruit that all gets ripe at once. Meat can also be processed into jerky this way, if it is very lean.

Our dehydrading unit has four trays and a thermostat control for various kinds of foods.

If you live in a somewhat dry climate, you can use a solar dehydrator, which uses no electricity. Or, just set out your food on elevated screen material in the sun, which is how raisins are made in California, and how people in Central Asia dry apples.

A variation of dehydrating is to **make the dehydrated**

food into a powder. This saves a lot of space and is useful for foods that you often use as a paste or sauce anyway, such as tomatoes. If you like to make smoothies with your fruit, you can make very well-dried fruit into a powder in a blender or food processor.

Another variety of dried food is represented by pemmican, hardtack and Scottish bannocks. Pemmican was invented by native Americans and consists of dried and powdered lean meat, suet (rendered animal fat), and dried powdered berries. The ingredients are mixed and formed into small bars or cakes and then baked at low temperature to make sure they are completely devoid of moisture. Hardtack was invented for British sailors of the 18th century and consists simply of wheat cakes that are baked like pemmican. Bannocks consist of oatmeal, barley flour, butter, and water, which are also formed into small cakes and baked like the others. Pemmican and bannocks, having some oil in them, are somewhat water resistant and are tastier than hardtack, which will spoil if exposed to water. Hardtack also contains very little protein. One Scot who enjoys making his own trail food makes a combination of all three of these, which he calls a Fandabi Bannock.[2] The result is probably somewhat like Elven Lembas bread, for Lord of the Rings fans, in that one four-inch square only one finger thick is very filling.

A **cooler** can be used for short-term storage in off-grid situations in a dry climate. It can easily be constructed using a metal or plastic box covered with a burlap bag. A container on the top of the box slowly drips water on the bag, cooling the box by evaporation. In the early 20th century, most people in North America used these before they had refriger-

---

2. https://www.youtube.com/watch?v=V0cxV2vVC0U&t=977s

ators. These coolers can keep vegetables, cheese, butter, and other foods cool but not cold.

Using Winter Temperatures: if you live in a colder climate, you can use the outside air temperature for food storage—to cool food in the fall and spring and freeze it in the winter. You must just construct a box to contain the food, which will not allow any of your neighboring creatures to eat the food before you do. An ideal place would be a second-story window on the north side of your house. That way you can access the food easily by opening the window, and it will stay plenty cold (or frozen) in the shade. If you construct it out of wire mesh, birds will not be able to bother your stash. I have observed people in the former Soviet Union doing this as a regular practice.

Savings from this step that can be invested: A modest savings can be attained by this level, depending upon how many prepared foods you used to eat.

LEVEL 2: MORE DIFFICULT RECIPES; CANNING, PICKLING, AND FERMENTING

Cooking: This level involves preparing **foods that are somewhat more difficult or time-consuming to prepare,** but also are much cheaper to prepare than to buy already prepared in the supermarket. These include but are not at all limited to tamales, enchiladas, chile rellenos, dishes made with stuffed pasta (Italian ravioli or cannelloni, Chinese pot stickers, Russian pelmeni and vareniki, etc.); lasagna; stuffed grape leaves, cabbage, or peppers; baklava; and various kinds of cookies and cakes. Recipes are available on the internet.

Canning: At Level 2 for preserving, you can invest in your resilience by canning your own food, particularly if you have some fruit trees or a good-sized garden. This requires an investment in canning jars and lids and a large pot for sterilizing the jars before filling them. It also takes an investment of time—an hour or so to make a run of a particular product. Most fruits and vegetables can be canned, and there are many books and online resources for finding out how to do this safely and effectively - our favorite in listed in Appendix 2. It saves money because you buy the fruit or vegetables in the summer when they are plentiful and therefore cheaper. A bonus is that you can preserve the excess fruit and vegetables that you grow yourself and cannot eat during the season, and you can avoid the excess salt and sugar that are often in canned foods from the store.

Meat can also be canned, and corned beef is an example. It involves immersing the beef in a mixture of salt, nitrates (optional), sugar and pickling spices for about 10 days before canning in the brine.

Pickling is a form of canning in which the item is preserved in vinegar or by anaerobic fermentation in brine. Cucumbers are the most popular, so we call them simply "pickles." Many other vegetables can also be preserved this way, including cabbage (sauerkraut or kimchi), carrots, turnips, onions, cauliflower, and peppers. Buy these vegetables in the late summer when they are cheap and preserve them for the winter and spring. They are very tasty, and you can add spices to the brine for extra flavor. Again, you can avoid excessive salt in your diet by doing it yourself. Many recipes are available on the internet, and the process is not difficult.

The **processing of olives** is related to these but somewhat different and is also not difficult. The **traditional method**, which I have used, involves soaking the olives in a salt brine in a bucket or large jar for at least one month. You must put a plate on top of the olives to keep them submerged under the brine. Do not panic if a scum develops on top of the water—this is normal. The brine changes the chemistry of the raw olive so that the bitterness is removed. The olives are then canned in a weaker salt solution, to which spices like garlic or pepper can be added to taste. They will keep in this state for several years without refrigeration.

A **quicker method**, which I have also used, involves soaking the olives in lye, which is sold as drain cleaner at your hardware store! Be sure to obtain pure lye without other ingredients like those added to Drano and similar brands. The soaking in a lye solution takes only 12 to 24 hours, after which they can be rinsed several times and canned in salty water, as above. The taste will be different than the traditional method—more like the canned olives you buy in the supermarket, which have undoubtedly been processed in this way.

If you live in an area where olives are grown, try processing them yourself after looking up detailed directions (see Appendix 2). In some regions, olive trees are popular as yard beautification in apartment complexes because large, mature olive trees can easily be transplanted, creating an established look immediately after the complex has been constructed. They are also frost and drought-tolerant. Unless the trees are treated to prevent fruit from developing, the olives just fall to the ground and are wasted as well as making a mess on sidewalks. Ask the management if you can help them keep the area clean by harvesting them. Olives become ripe around November in most places where they are grown in the northern hemisphere.

Fermentation is a way to preserve grain or fruit juice, turning them into **beer and wine**. Very little specialized equipment is needed, but the process does take some practice. One key part of the process is controlling the temperature of the fermenting liquid, which varies according to what you are making. U.S. government rules allow you to make up to 200 gallons of beer or wine for your own use. Even more than with other foods, the savings is substantial because beer and wine from the store are heavily taxed. You will need a jug or container and a siphon or other device that keeps oxygen out of the fermentation container but allows the carbon dioxide created by the process to escape.

Related to this is the turning of milk into **kefir**, using a lactobacillus culture. Kefir keeps much longer than milk and, being probiotic, is good for you. The process is not difficult —you simply put a starter culture in some milk and leave it in a jar on your kitchen counter covered loosely. In a few days, your kefir is ready, and you can preserve it in the refrigerator. In the market, kefir costs about two to three times as much as milk, so making it yourself will save money. To keep your culture alive, you must continue to feed it fresh milk, so if you go on a trip, you will need a friend to babysit your culture.

Kombucha is also a fermented drink made from tea and sugar. Yeast is added, which turns the sugar into alcohol, but bacteria are also added, which turn the alcohol into vinegar. The result is a slightly fizzy, tart, probiotic beverage with the flavor of the tea you used. You need a large open jar and some starter material, like for making kefir or yogurt. This starter culture is called a SCOBY, meaning a symbiotic culture of bacteria and yeast. Unlike beer and wine, kombucha is fermented in open or loosely covered containers, but like beer and wine, the temperature plays a key role. Kombucha can be purchased in many urban areas, but it is somewhat expensive, so if you like it and want to drink a lot of it, it could be worth your while to make your own. You will need to find a small piece of

SCOBY to start, and a container made of glass or food-grade plastic.

Savings from this step that can be invested: Savings can be substantial if you currently enjoy canned, pickled, or fermented foods.

LEVEL 3: COOKING TOTALLY FROM SCRATCH, ROOT CELLARS, ICE HOUSES, SMOKING AND CURING

Cooking Totally from Scratch: At this level, you are starting with raw, unprocessed food of all kinds. You could be slaughtering your own meat, obtaining raw milk from cows or goats, and grinding your own flour from different grains. You would be preserving your extra food during the summer and fall, and eating it in the winter. In truth, you are "homesteading out on the prairie," and this level is particularly for those who are not only off the grid (Chapter 1) but out of regular contact with civilization altogether.

Example: Village life in the former Soviet Union. In the 1990s, I visited a village in Kazakhstan with a former resident. We were invited into a house and were treated to a small meal, as the culture dictated. We had bread, butter, cheese, jam, eggs, potatoes, tomatoes, cucumbers with dill, and various berries and fruit. The owner of the house explained that everything on the table came from her own small yard. She only went to the village store (a short walk away) about twice a year, and then only for flour, sugar, and tea. The economy at that time was in a shambles—there was no work for anyone, especially in villages, and the village store (which I saw) had very little to sell other than flour, sugar, and tea. But the people were resilient and survived by growing, preserving, and cooking nearly everything themselves.

Root cellars are at Level 3 because many homes do not have a climate or an existing house cellar where this is feasible. You must live in a climate with cold winters, where the cellar will be be between 45 and 55 degrees during the winter, but not freeze. It must also be between 80 and 90% humidity—that is, not so damp so that the food rots and not so dry so that the food shrivels and dries out. Most importantly, it must be dark and have some ventilation so that the ethylene gas from ripening fruit does not build up, which causes fruit to ripen too fast and vegetables to rot.

Some people add an underground storage room outside their house, if the house does not already have a suitable cellar, or the cellar has been converted to other uses. Other places for a root cellar might include the crawlspace below a house, under a porch or deck on the north side of a house, or in an unheated outbuilding or garage. Sometimes a closet on the north side of the inside of a house will work. You would have to check the temperature in there.

For a **simple root cellar**, some people bury a trash can in the ground in a shady area so that only a few inches are showing above the ground. Holes are drilled in the bottom and a rack system put inside. The regular lid is used with a few small holes, making sure it is a tight fit so that animals cannot get in. It is a little cumbersome getting items from the bottom, but the rack can be built with a handle so it can be lifted out. It is a very cheap way to create a root cellar if other locations are not available. See Appendix 2 for links to detailed instructions.

Root crops such as potatoes, carrots, beets, and onions would be placed in the cellar just as they come from the field, without washing. The dirt covering them keeps microbes away, and washing can create small cuts in them which let microbes in. Washing can also leave them too wet so that they rot. Cabbage can also be stored for several months. In addition, low-moisture cheeses can be stored this way, as well as preserved or cured meats such as hard salami. Make sure that mice and other critters do not have access, or you will lose your food!

The best kind of fruit for a cellar are apples, especially Granny Smith and other tart varieties. For best results, pack the fruit in straw, dry leaves, or newspapers so that they are not touching each other directly. That way, if one starts to spoil, the spoilage will not spread to the others as quickly. Do not use plastic containers like tubs, which retain too much moisture and ethylene gas, but rather wooden or cardboard boxes. Pears, pomegranates, and some other temperate-climate fruit can also be stored in a cellar, but not for as long as apples.

Ice houses are used similarly to root cellars. They are suitable for northern climates where you can easily accumulate a good quantity of ice during the winter and store it in the ice house, packed in wood chips or sawdust.

Curing and smoking meat and fish is a specialized process that takes months to complete. It involves drying the meat or fish using salt and/or sodium nitrate, hanging it up to dry until it is half its original weight, and then smoking it over a very slow, smoky fire. You can invest in smokers that are about the size of a barbecue grill but taller, or construct a wooden smokehouse for larger quantities.

The **return on investment** in smoking meat could be questioned. Certainly, the value of the smoked meat is much higher than the raw product, but raw meat can more easily be preserved in a large freezer, powered by solar panels. A hundred and fifty years ago, many animals were often slaughtered in the fall, so that they would not have to be fed and housed in a barn through the winter. For that large quantity of meat to be preserved, it had to be turned into cured sausage or dried and cured like a ham because there was no refrigeration. Nowadays, cows, pigs, and chickens are slaughtered at about the same rate year-round, so the price stays about the same, unlike fruits and vegetables, which go in and out of season and thus up and down in price. Even if you go hunting and bag a deer or other large animal, or you go ocean fishing and catch a good quantity of large fish, you can put the meat or fish into a large chest-style freezer, powered by your own solar panels with a battery backup.

Therefore, while curing and smoking meat and fish is a worthwhile hobby, unless you live in a rural, very remote location, it would be hard to count it as a practical investment in resilience as long as the electric grid stays functioning.

Extra bonus: Food that you have prepared and preserved yourself is healthier! There will be no unnecessarily added salt, sugar, or chemicals. Most store-bought prepared food, and particularly cured meat and fish, has unhealthy chemicals, although more low-sodium, low-sugar food is now available in specialty markets.

Saivngs from this step that can be invested: If you have a large garden, this step is a must to preserve your harvest and your savings. It will significantly reduce your food budget even if you buy the fruit and vegetables in the market but during the season rather than in the off-season.

CHAPTER 6
WATER

We never know the worth of
water till the well is dry.
Thomas Fuller, 1658–1734

BE PREPARED FOR DROUGHT

Periodically, there are droughts around the world, and in the southwestern states of North America in particular. They say that the entire Colorado River watershed has been in a drought condition for the past 20 years—the worst mega-drought of the past 1200 years.[1] It is now worse than the drought that caused the cliff dwellings at Mesa Verde, Colorado to become uninhabited.[2] If this weather pattern does not change, the lives of the 40 million people who depend on this basin for water will be severely impacted. It

1. https://www.washingtonpost.com/climate-environment/2023/02/05/colorado-river-drought-explained/, https://labs.waterdata.usgs.gov/visualizations/OWDI-drought/en/index.html
2. https://coloradosun.com/2022/02/14/tree-ring-drought-1200-years-colorado-southwest/#:

would also impact the rest of the people in North America because a significant amount of vegetables eaten during the winter come from farms watered by the lower Colorado River basin.

In 1977, there was a drought in the whole state of California, and I visited friends in an urban area that were required to use no more than 20 gallons (80 liters) of water per person per day. This was total use for all purposes—drinking, cooking, toilet flushing, and washing bodies, dishes, and clothes. Watering of lawns was prohibited, as was the washing of cars. Twenty gallons sounds like a lot, but it is not, compared with our current use patterns. The average American now uses between 80 and 100 gallons (320 to 400 liters) of water daily.[3] How would you fare if you had to use only 20 gallons? Take a look at your monthly use of water on your bill, divide by the number of people in your household, and see.

Temporary Droughts

In addition to decades-long severe drought situations, there are other less chronic conditions. If there were a **prolonged blackout**, your municipal water supply may run out due to lack of power for pumps. This happened in some areas of Texas during the big freeze of February 2021.[4] Over one million people in Houston either did not have water or

3. https://www.usgs.gov/special-topics/water-science-school/science/water-qa-how-much-water-do-i-use-home-each-day

4. The beginning of this video explains how the blackout in Texas in February 2021 caused a lack of water pressure, thus compromising its purity, and thus encouraging this homeowner to install a large rainwater tank: https://www.youtube.com/watch?v=cuu3e3t-qlc

were told to boil it first.[5] Many others had no water in their house because pipes burst due to the cold. In a hurricane or flood, the municipal supply may become contaminated. What would you do if you could not use your tap water for drinking or cooking for three days? For a week? For a month?

If you are outside city limits, you most likely are already providing your own water supply with a well. To be resilient in this situation, you would need to provide ahead for a power outage that would then cut off the power for your pump. See Chapter 1 for how to be resilient in electric power.

If you are inside city limits and rely on a municipal water supply, then it would be impractical as well as illegal in many places to supply your own water with a well. Anything you do in this case to assure an alternate source of water supply for drinking and cooking in case of emergency would therefore be more in the nature of "prepping" rather than investing in resilience, since you would not be using this alternate source for normal drinking, cooking, and cleaning.

Nevertheless, everyone should have 3 gallons of **emergency bottled water** for each person in their family, stored in a cool location out of sunlight. You can buy gallon containers cheaply in a discount market and store them in your garage or in the back of a closet. Remember to use them each year and buy new ones, so they are fresh. Mark them clearly with the month and year you bought them to remind you. These would be used in case an earthquake, hurricane, tornado, or other disaster were to damage the municipal fresh water system temporarily.

You should also have a method to filter, chemically treat,

---

5. https://www.nytimes.com/2021/02/20/us/texas-winter-storm-explainer.html

and/or boil water in case the municipal water were contaminated for a long period of time. The best way to do this would be a small backpacking water filter because it takes only a few minutes and does not require fuel for boiling. In an emergency, water can be sterilized by ultraviolet light from the sun by putting the water into a clear plastic bottle in strong sunlight for at least six hours. This does not get rid of harmful chemicals, however. These are all practical "prepping" steps but not investments, since you would not be using these steps on a day-to-day basis to save on your water bill.

Economizing on Water in Normal Times

However, you can certainly invest in some items to economize on the water that you do receive from your water utility, particularly if you live in an older home where these measures have not been taken in the past. You can also filter your own drinking water, rather than buy it.

As far as watering your plants and garden and other non-drinking uses, there are several alternative sources. These would reduce your water bill each year, and therefore can be counted as an investment in resilience. In addition to reducing your own expenses, these steps increase the resilience of your community as a whole. Large parts of the Western United States, as well as huge swaths of the world as a whole, suffer from a deficit of fresh water. Any steps that you can take which ease this shortage is a step toward solving this problem for your community.

With the exception of washing machines, most of these steps do not involve buying products with parts from overseas, so they will not be disrupted by supply chain issues.

LEVEL 1: ECONOMIZE, DRINKING WATER FILTRATION, SIMPLE CISTERNS, EASY GRAY WATER, MINOR SOURCES

Economize: Your first investment in water resilience is to economize your present use. Invest in a water-saving shower head that uses no more than 2 gallons per minute, if you don't already have one. Invest also in low water use toilets, which use only 1.6 gallons per flush. Toilets from the 80s and earlier use about 3.5 gallons per flush, and those from the 60s and earlier use about 5 gallons, so the newer toilets will definitely save water. Economize in your yard and garden as well. If you live in an area subject to drought, plant only drought-tolerant ornamental plants, and use a drip system, soaker hose, or wicking containers for your garden (see Chapter 5). This saves a lot of water compared with letting water flow down furrows or using sprinklers.

Filter Your Own Drinking Water: If you are in the habit of buying bottled drinking water, consider investing in your own filter.

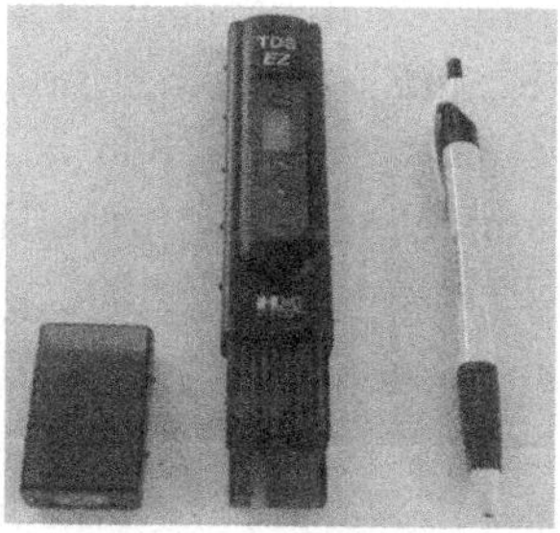

First, invest in a small instrument that measures the particulate count of your water, measured in parts per million (ppm). They are often called a **TDS meter** (total dissolved solids), and cost $12 to $15—see my photo at right, compared with a pen. In an area where the water has less than 150 ppm of dissolved solids, usually a pitcher with a simple drop-in **particle and charcoal filter** will be sufficient, such as a Brita. It will take out the chlorine and other unpleasant elements and tastes. However, if your water has more than 150 ppm of dissolved material, then you might consider a more expensive drop-in filter system, such as ZeroWater, or a **reverse osmosis filter** system for the water you use for drinking and cooking. Over the long term, this will be much easier, cheaper, and more efficient than buying drinking water in throw-away plastic containers. Berkey water filters are also popular and work just with gravity, although they are somewhat bulky and a little expensive. There are instructions on the internet for how to make your own Berkey-type filter containers. You would then just buy the replacement filters rather than the complete system.

Simple Cisterns: You can also take simple measures to collect your own water for nonpotable uses. It is a simple matter to install a rain barrel for each downspout from your roof.

These can be purchased at many hardware stores. Elevate these barrels with bricks or boards, so that the faucet outlet near the bottom is at least 8 to 12 inches off the ground. This allows you to put a container under the faucet to fill it. It also allows you to attach a hose to that faucet and water any part of your yard that is below the level of the faucet. Remember that water is heavy—it weighs about 8.3 pounds per gallon. Therefore a 40-gallon (160 liter) rain barrel will weigh about 415 pounds (189 kg) when it is full, so do not place this barrel on

My own 50 gallon rain barrel below a downspout

loose soil—it will compact the soil and the barrel will lean or sink.

If you use a barrel that was not made to use as a rain collector, then make sure that you cover the top with a fine screen or other material to keep out mosquitoes.

The economic utility of the rain barrels will depend on how often it rains where you live, and how expensive your municipal water is. During long dry spells (many months in dry areas of Western states), it will not be used very much. The formula for how much water you will collect in a month is the square feet of roof, times the monthly rainfall in inches, times a factor of 0.62, times 75%–90% to allow for wastage. This will give you the amount of water in gallons.

Some cities are encouraging people to collect rainwater because it reduces the amount of water the city has to deal with in a large rainstorm. Cities in Australia, Kenya, China, Brazil, and Thailand practice large-scale rainwater harvesting. The airport in Frankfurt, Germany, uses rainwater for flushing toilets and landscaping. In Texas, where the western half of the state is rather dry, there is a tax exemption for the expenses of harvesting rainwater.[6]

Besides watering your garden, this collected water can be used for swimming pools and hot tubs; for car washing; for water features in your yard such as fountains, bird baths, and ponds; and for watering your pets and livestock. Since rainwater does not contain any dissolved minerals, it will be better for your pool, which otherwise will concentrate minerals over a period of years due to evaporation. Every gallon you collect with your rain barrels reduces the amount you pay your water utility and helps your community as a whole save water. In a period of severe drought, this water

6. https://www.twdb.texas.gov/publications/brochures/conservation/doc/RainwaterHarvestingManual_3rdedition.pdf

could also be used for flushing your toilet. But do not use this water for drinking or cooking, because it could contain bird droppings and other contaminants from your roof.

In a disaster situation, these rain barrels become your emergency water supply. If you are able to filter this water with a backpacker's water filter, you then have enough water for drinking and cooking to last for weeks. If the disaster were to happen during or immediately after the rainy season, you will have an emergency supply at hand.

Easy Gray Water: The other step you can take easily is to use gray water. In many homes, it is a relatively simple matter to route the drain hose of your washing machine into a hose that would lead outside to your garden. If that is not practical in your situation, you can direct that water into a large bucket. If you use biodegradable soap in your washer, it will not harm most plants, particularly trees. During one of the droughts that periodically plague California, I have observed people use this water to flush their toilets.

Other Minor Sources: Air Conditioner Condensation If you have an air conditioner, water condenses on the cooling tubes, drips down into a pan, and is usually conducted to a drain or outside through a small tube. You can collect this water and use it on your garden, rather than just let it go down a drain, particularly during the hot summer months when you are running the air conditioner.[7] In the Southeast, where the weather is hot and humid, the amount of water collected from this source is substantial. Some commercial

---

7. https://www.gardeningknowhow.com/garden-how-to/watering/is-irrigating-with-ac-water-safe.htm

establishments are starting to utilize this resource.[8] Since it condenses from water in the air, it does not contain any salts that would harm your plants or animals. But for human consumption, it should be run through a sterilizing process.

Reverse Osmosis Waste Water: If you have a reverse osmosis water filter system, it will send about 20% of the water down an adjacent drain—water that contains the salts and other dissolved solids that have been filtered out. This water, if collected, would be too salty for watering your plants but could certainly be used for flushing your toilets, if you really needed to save water. For example, a local company that makes kombucha has an industrial-sized reverse osmosis system. The waste water from this system is fed into an elevated tank, which is the source of water for the toilets in their facility.

Savings from this step that can be invested: You will save only a little on your water bill, but in drought times you will have water for your garden and other outside uses when others do not.

LEVEL 2: FRONT-LOADING WASHING MACHINES, LARGE CISTERNS, AND GRAY WATER SYSTEMS

Saving Water with Front-loading Washing Machines: This is included at Level 2 because washing machines are relatively expensive. So, when you need to replace your

8. https://www.watertechonline.com/water-reuse/article/15550318/the-benefits-of-harvesting-hvac-condensation

machine, consider getting a front-loader. The typical top-loader uses from 30 to 40 gallons of water to wash and rinse a load of laundry, while the typical front-loader only requires 10 to 15 gallons for the same function. So, the savings of water is substantial. As a bonus, because there is no agitator in the middle, there is less wear and tear on your clothes, and they will last longer.

Large Cisterns: If you have a large yard, you may be able to purchase a large tank and position it so that the water from all your roof gutters would flow into it. This would give you hundreds, or perhaps thousands of gallons of water for the uses listed in Level 1—water you do not have to purchase from your local utility. A local nursery/hardware store in our neighborhood uses this strategy to water their many plants.

A large cistern would also be useful for fighting fires, if it were combined with an off-grid pump.

In addition to these uses, if you would like to invest in some plumbing, you could have your toilets flush with this free water. If you added a simple filter, it could also be used for washing your clothes. But you would not want to use this water for drinking or cooking unless you installed a high level of filtration and purification. You would also want to install a "first flush diverter" which diverts the first part of any rainfall away from your cistern, because it may contain bird droppings and other contaminants. One man in the Tucson area gets nearly all the water he uses in this fashion, and that area gets only 4.6 inches (11.5 cm) of rain per year.[9]

Piping Gray Water: If your home is built up on a foundation, you can go in the crawl space and reroute the drain pipes from your showers and sinks to go into your garden. I have done this, and I am not a plumber! But do not do this with your kitchen sink because you will be putting food scraps there that could cause a stink in your garden, indicating bacteria that you do not want among your vegetables. In general, it is better to use gray water on trees and not on vegetables. This puts some distance between any possible bacteria and something you will be eating. For trees, direct the pipe of gray water into a 4 to 6 inch diameter plastic pipe at least 10 to15 feet long that has small holes drilled along the bottom and both ends closed. Bury this pipe at least 6 inches below the soil, near the roots of your trees. When someone drains a bathtub of water, it flows into this large pipe and from there slowly drains into the soil, watering your trees.

Bonus: If your house has a septic system, diverting gray water from it to your garden increases the "retention rate" of the waste water that flows into your septic tank. That is, the average amount of time that water stays in that tank is increased. This allows the bacteria in there more time to break down the waste and prolongs the life of your system—especially the leach field. If your leach field becomes clogged with solid matter, it must be replaced, which means digging a new one in another location of your yard at a cost

9. https://www.youtube.com/watch?v=KcAMXm9zITg&t=2080s

of thousands of dollars. I had that unfortunate experience before we diverted the gray water to our garden.

Savings from this step that can be invested: You will save significant amounts on your water bill in drought-prone areas. In addition, you may avoid an expensive repair of your septic system.

LEVEL 3: PERMACULTURE OR EARTHSHIP, FOG HARVESTING, ATMOSPHERIC WATER GENERATORS

Permaculture/Earthship: This level is much better and easier when it's designed into the house to start with rather than added later. In this system, all water is used at least two, three, or even four times, and the result is a dwelling that uses very little, if any, water from the "outside."

Rainwater → coarse particulate filter → cistern → fine filtration & sanitation → sinks, showers, and laundry → indoor greenhouse with solid floor and overflow collector → toilets → septic tank → leach field next to orchard.

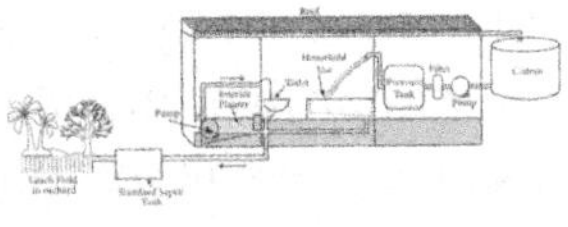

Diagram of a Permaculture/Earthship water system by arafat_creative through fiverr.com

Rainwater is first collected from the roof and is directed down to a large cistern. On the way, it passes through filters that keep out leaves, animals, and debris. The water in the cistern is then put through a fine filter and ultraviolet or filter sanitation before being distributed to the various sinks, showers, and the laundry. The outflow of the washing machine and the sinks (except the kitchen) is directed to the indoor greenhouse, which has a rubber-lined solid bottom. A sump in the greenhouse collects any excess water, which has been filtered by the soil and the plants. Water from the sump is pumped to supply the toilet. The waste from the toilet as well as the kitchen sink goes into a standard septic tank, which has a standard set of leach lines. But these leach lines are located next to a small orchard, which is thereby watered. Thus most of the water is used four times—in a sink or shower, in the indoor greenhouse, to flush the toilet, and to water the orchard.

It is very likely that many of these elements will become standard features of houses in the future, particularly in arid regions. Population pressures will force us to make more efficient use of the water that is available to us. Some regions, such as the town of Cambria in California, already do not allow any more connections to the municipal system, or any new wells to be drilled, because the system and the aquifer are already over-subscribed.

Fog Harvesting: There are some regions that are arid but have cool nights with fog from a nearby ocean. In these places, it is possible to erect "fog-catchers"—large vertical plastic nets with a trough and a container underneath to collect the water that condenses on the nets, particularly at night. The fog catcher producers say it is possible to collect hundreds of liters of water nightly from only one sheet measuring ten feet square. These are being used now in Peru, Morocco, the Canary Islands, and other places for communities that have no access to water. One researcher is working on a more effective model which uses vertical strings rather than a net so that the water droplets do not hang up on the horizontal elements of a net. He calls it a "water harp." The beauty of such a system is that it requires no energy or human attention, and can be produced cheaply. People in some coastal areas of California might benefit and become more resilient through this strategy. See Appendix 2, Chapter 6 for video links and details.

Atmospheric Water Generators (AWG): Some companies are now producing small appliances about the size of an office water cooler that take water out of the air through refrigeration. These use a significant amount of electricity—most models use about 400 watt-hours to produce a liter of water. One unit, the WaterGen, claims increased efficiency of 310 watt-hours per liter at 60% humidity by using a heat exchanger.[10] An AWG would only be a good investment in resilience if you lived in an area with little or no fresh water or rainfall but near an ocean where it is very humid and the units could work with maximum efficiency, such as coastal Southern and Central California. These units cost about $1,800, and produce 5 liters per day when the humidity is 50%, and more than 10 liters per day if the humidity is 80%. Some companies produce larger units for producing more water, but are, of course, even more expensive.

Another type of AWG is one that is integrated with a solar panel, so that it does not add to your electric bill, or can be used in an off-grid situation. "Hydropanels" have been created by an Arizona company called Source, and have been reviewed by a YouTuber.[11] He found that if the $6,000 cost were spread out over five years, it would produce seven liters (1.8 gallons) per day and would cost 20 cents per liter

---

10. https://us.watergen.com/

11. https://www.thecooldown.com/green-home/hydropanels-work-build-yourself-kitchen/

(90 cents per gallon). At this cost, such a gadget, like the one above, would only be practical in an area with no access to well water and little rainfall but plentiful sun and humidity.

Savings from this step that can be invested: At this level you may be able to avoid any water bill at all and have water when others in your arid region do not

Potential new technologies: Because of the ongoing droughts around the world, researchers have been busy working on new methods of producing fresh water for individuals as well as for communities. For example, researchers at MIT are working on a small suitcase-sized "ion concentration polarization" unit that would produce 0.3 liter per hour while using only 20 watts per liter. They estimate that the unit would cost only about $50.[12]

Researchers at DARPA have come up with a gel that absorbs water from the air, made from ordinary materials that would cost about $2 per kilogram. It absorbs water at ordinary temperatures but releases it when heated. They say that 1 kilogram could produce 6 liters per day at 15% humidity and 13 liters per day at 30% humidity.[13] These are very dry conditions and underline their objective of creating a method of collecting water for soldiers operating in the desert. The lifespan of both these methods are not yet known, and neither is ready for commercial production. If a machine could be produced that would use solar power for

12. https://dspace.mit.edu/handle/1721.1/123424
13. https://insights.globalspec.com/article/18757/darpa-funded-gel-film-pulls-water-from-air#:

the required heat, then this could be used by ordinary civilians living in desert conditions.

CONCLUSION FOR HOUSING (CHAPTERS 1-6):

Resilient Location

A house should not be located in an area unduly subject to fires, floods, hurricanes, or tornadoes unless the house is particularly designed to withstand those dangers. Insurance companies have paid people to rebuild their houses after floods in recent years numerous times in the exact same location and in the same way. The federal government rebuilds infrastructure after storms the same way.[14] This is non-resilient insanity.

As a counter example, one man on the Gulf Coast of Florida resolved to be different and built his house to withstand a hurricane. His specifications were way beyond what was required by the local building code in terms of height of the house above the designated flood level, and strength to withstand wind damage. Sure enough, a few years later a hurricane came through and wiped out all his neighbors, but his house stood firm and virtually undamaged by water or wind.[15]

What to Look For in an Existing House

Outside:

1. Orientation and layout: more windows facing the

---

14. https://www.nytimes.com/2012/11/19/science/earth/as-coasts-rebuild-and-us-pays-again-critics-stop-to-ask-why.html
15. https://www.foxblocks.com/blog/home-construction-built-endure-hurricanes

winter sun, fewer on the other sides. Solar panels already installed, or a convenient place to install them.

2. Mature fruit trees and a place for a garden, if a single family residence.

3. If a condo, a patio or balcony with significant sun exposure.

Inside:

1. The more insulation, the better, particularly in more extreme climates (hot or cold).

2. Windows are double pane or better.

3. Appliances are high efficiency (Energy Star).

4. If in a cold climate, the fireplace has an insert, or there is a free-standing, efficient fireplace.

Strive to Improve your Resilience

If you are at the ultimate level for everything in Chapters 1-6, then you are totally off the grid and self-sufficient in shelter, energy, food, and water, thus making you very resilient. This is difficult to attain unless you have a good amount of property—minimum several acres, depending on climate, terrain, and soil type. But any increase in your resilience in any area will be a great help to you and your community.

On the other hand, if you have several acres of land, this usually means you are some distance away from stores and services, thus subtracting from your transportation resilience (Chapter 7), and perhaps your ability to network with others (Chapter 12). Choose the balance that works best for you.

The Ultimate: Earthships

One example of what ultimate resilience could look like is the "Earthship" design. An Earthship is a trademarked, state-of-the-art, self-sustainable, off-grid building that follows six basic principles, covering six basic human needs by:

1. Building with natural and repurposed (recycled) materials such as used tires, discarded bottles and cans, and dirt and rocks from the property where it is located or the immediate vicinity.
2. Heating and cooling as needed through proper window placement, thermal mass, and natural ventilation to create a comfortable living environment (passive heating and cooling). Usually, no outside energy is needed for this purpose.
3. Producing wind and/or solar energy on-site to create any electricity that is needed.
4. Harvesting and filtering rainwater to provide all the water required by the house and gardens.
5. Containing and treating its own waste water without external contamination.
6. Producing its own food in an integrated greenhouse and gardens.

The classic Earthship has a large earthen berm on the north side (in the northern hemisphere) and curving around to both the east and west sides. This berm gives the house a large thermal mass, which moderates the large swings in temperature between day and night and between summer and winter in continental climates.

Following the first principle, this berm is usually constructed out of worn-out tires from a dump, filled with earth from the site. These tires are generally free, and in some cases, they might even pay you to take them away. Some walls are made to include old cans and bottles. The multi-colored bottles are placed horizontally in the walls, and make otherwise solid adobe or cob walls very attractive by letting some light through in artistic patterns.

The south side of an Earthship is covered with windows, sometimes tilted so that the winter sun is perpendicular to the glass, thus allowing the entrance of a maximum amount of heat and light at that time of year. The square footage of the glass should be 30% of the square footage of the house, so that the house is adequately heated during the winter. The roof of the Earthship is designed to collect precipitation and direct it to cisterns, where it can be used inside.

Since the main structural element usually consists of earth-filled old tires, Earthships are resistant to natural disasters such as hurricanes, tornadoes, forest fires, and earthquakes. They are also resistant to termites, since wood is used only in some interior walls and cabinets and in roof supports.

The Earthship concept was created by Mike Reynolds and is carried forward by the Earthship Biotecture organization. See Appendix 2 for links and more details.

Earthship Design Adapted to Local Climate

Since the Earthship concept originated in Taos, New Mexico, which has a dry, continental climate, the design described above has been made for that climate. In that climate, wide swings in temperature and the relative lack of water dictate its form and features. Earthships that have been constructed in tropical places such as Puerto Rico or Central Africa are quite different. In those areas, a large thermal mass is not needed, nor are greenhouses, nor is the reuse of water resources so critical. Instead, the design is oriented around passive cooling through dome shapes, with a way for heat to escape through the top. The use of solar panels for electricity, and the collection of water from the roof is the same in both cases. Earthships in much colder and/or wetter climates need to deal with the potential for condensation to form on the inside walls, causing mold, and the possible need for supplemental heating.

See the appendix for links to the Earthship Biotecture organization in Taos, as well as the building of an Earthship in Florida, which has a very different design due to its tropical location.

Drawbacks of Earthships

One of the main drawbacks of the original Earthship design is that packing used tires with earth is a very labor-intensive process. The earth must be rammed into the tire with a large, heavy hammer so that the tire will support a lot of weight on it without sagging or compacting. One observer said that a strong, healthy person could only pack about eight tires in a day, and a normally sized Earthship requires about 800 to 900 earth-filled tires.[16] Thus, just the tire-packing part of construction requires about 100 man-days of labor, or 800 man-hours, not including the time needed to select that many similar-sized tires from a dump and transport them to your site. To solve this problem, the Earthship proponents offer hands-on training for would-be Earthship builders, in which the trainees actually construct an entire Earthship from the ground up. Thus, nearly all Earthships are built with massive amounts of volunteer labor.

In addition to being labor intensive, the use of tires in a residential building has come under question due to fears

---

16. https://www.youtube.com/watch?v=Si9DpgSy1EE&t=6s

that the tires could release toxins into the air or the ground.[17] This potential has not been proved or disproved, but due to this, some builders are now using alternative ways to create the berm, as discussed below.

One of the stated attractions of the Earthship design is the use of recycled materials such as old tires, aluminum cans, and glass bottles. However, the use of cans and bottles, in most cases, removes them from the recycling stream, where they would otherwise be made into new cans and bottles. All three of these items must be transported to the construction site, usually from some distance away. The use of these materials requires much labor, thus raising the expense of the building even further.

Even with volunteer labor, Earthships are not easy or cheap to construct, in large part because many of the components are custom made on-site. One source estimated that Earthships cost between $150 and $225 per square foot, which is significantly more than a standard house.[18]

Another disadvantage of Earthships is that the large area required by the berm means that the whole house has a footprint of 3,500 square feet, even though the interior contains less than 2,000 square feet. This means that it needs a minimum lot size of 1 acre, which increases the cost and further constrains where one can be built.

Some have proposed constructing the berm/thermal storage out of more conventional materials such as concrete blocks, but these would significantly add to the cost and sidestep the goal of using recycled or natural materials. Concrete also releases a significant amount of carbon dioxide into the atmosphere during the manufacturing

---

17. https://freedomresidence.com/are-the-tires-used-in-earthships-toxic-answered/
18. https://freedomresidence.com/how-much-do-earthships-actually-cost-to-build/

process. One observer suggested using the earthbag method, in which plastic tubes are filled with local dirt and anchored in place with rebar. Others have suggested using rammed earth, which is a proven construction technique. In any case, it is the earth inside a tire wall that provides the thermal mass and not the tires themselves, which simply provide a way to stabilize the berm. This is still a movement in process, and more alternatives will undoubtedly be developed.

A more general difficulty with Earthships is that they are definitely not standard building techniques, and local building departments are often not inclined to approve of them without much discussion, if they approve them at all. But this is slowly changing, as the wisdom of these techniques becomes more widely known. Earthships and Earthship-inspired homes are now being built around the world.

More Development Needed

More work needs to be done to apply Earthship principles to other climates, soil conditions, and housing situations. One design does not and can not fit for all. It would be very helpful if there were Earthship-type designs readily available to home builders in every climate zone and latitude, for example. There could also be designs for every size of dwelling, from studio apartments to four bedroom houses, as well as different compass and street orientations, small urban and suburban as well as large rural lots, and different styles of architecture. With standard but flexible designs, Earthships and Earthship design elements could become common in urban and suburban lots everywhere, as well as out in the New Mexico desert.

NEW DEVELOPMENTS TO LOOK FOR:

- New ways to retrofit water-saving elements into existing houses.
- New water-saving elements included as standard in new housing developments.
- Off-the-shelf designs for Earthship-type houses that could be built on a city or suburban lot.
- New methods of turning saltwater to fresh, drinkable water using electrical fields.

CHAPTER 7
TRANSPORTATION

Bicycles are the most efficient vehicles
on the planet, 50 times more efficient than cars,
and twice as efficient as walking.
Godo Stoyke

Fitting a walk into a busy life can be
challenging, so I suggest walking rather
than driving to work or running errands
as often as you can—in other words, think of
walking as alternative transportation.
Andrew Weil

Restore human legs as a means of travel.
Pedestrians rely on food for fuel
and need no special parking facilities.
Lewis Mumford

There is more to life than increasing its speed.
Mahatma Gandhi

WE WERE TOTALLY NOT RESILIENT

The gas crises of 1973 and 1978 were a long time ago, but they illustrated a lack of resilience in transportation. When certain OPEC countries stopped exporting oil to the West, a small shortfall of oil supply led to crude oil prices quadrupling, causing a doubling and then re-doubling of prices at the pump, and long lines to fill up. Most people simply had no way to travel other than by a car that would only get 13 miles per gallon. The U.S. is only slightly more resilient today, as shown by the May, 2021 shutdown of a major gasoline pipeline in a Southeastern state due to hackers. Cars now get an average of 23 miles per gallon, but any small disruption of the supply still causes huge problems because the demand is very inelastic. Necessary travel, such as to work or school, uses the vast majority of gasoline and diesel fuel, so consumers just pay whatever it takes to fill their tank, no matter the price.

What would you do if gasoline were suddenly unavailable for a week, or perhaps for a month or more? How would you go to work or to school? How could you obtain groceries? Go to your doctor? If you have no other way to get to those places other than a gasoline or diesel-powered car, then you are not resilient in the area of transportation. Even if you normally rely on public transportation, what would you do if this were not available for some reason, such as a strike or a failure of the electric grid? Working from home is an option for some people, but not for most service industries and factories where the worker must be on-site.

WHAT CAN WE DO?

Almost 17% of the average American family's budget is spent on transportation.[1] This includes the purchase of vehicles, maintenance and repair, insurance, license and registration, and of course, fuel. An individual person cannot make his own motor vehicle, and these days, it typically takes a specialist to even do any repair on a modern one. Regarding fuel, even if we had an oil well in our backyard, to make our own fuel would require a very complex refinery to "crack" the crude oil into its constituent parts, and even then, less than half of it would become gasoline. So we cannot fuel our car with gasoline we make at home, but we can **fuel it with electric power** we produce at home in the ways outlined in Chapter 1: Energy. And, we can transport ourselves short distances with much simpler vehicles such as **bicycles**.

With the recent development of better batteries and electric motors, there are myriad motorized transportation alternatives today beyond traditional cars that need gasoline or diesel. For transporting just yourself, in addition to the famous Segway, there are motorized skateboards of all sizes. There are scooters with and without seats, with regular or "fat tires," and some are fold-able. There are numerous "uniwheels" and many other conveyances on which one stands to ride. There are now many electric scooters or mopeds of the traditional Vespa style. Electrically assisted bicycles have many configurations, including different recumbent types with two, three, or four wheels, and some are even all-wheel drive. There are pedal-electric enclosed vehicles with three or four wheels. Electric motorcycles have made an entrance,

1. https://data.bts.gov/stories/s/ida7-k95k#transportation-expenditures-and-income

sized from small to large, powerful ones. Even Harley Davidson is now producing an electric model.[2]

Electric cars are now available that can carry one, two, four, or five passengers, in all sizes. There are electric and plug-in hybrid cars that can go more than 300 miles at a stretch. Many of these transportation alternatives are great fun to ride, and look extremely cool. One safety note: Three-wheeled vehicles with one wheel in front and two in the back are inherently unstable—they can easily tip over when making turns at even medium speeds, and should only be for lower speed travel unless they have an extremely low center of gravity. It was for this reason that ATVs with this configuration were banned in 1988.[3] Two wheels in front and one in the rear, in contrast, is nearly as stable as having four wheels.

MANY BENEFITS OF ELECTRIC VEHICLES

For all these electric vehicles, you can invest in your own resilience because **you provide the fuel** for yourself at home. As an added bonus, one of the characteristics of electric motors is that they have the same **torque** no matter what speed the motor is turning. This is in contrast with internal combustion engines (ICE), which have a torque curve—the engine must be turning at a particular speed to create maximum power. Thus, electric vehicles generally have **fast initial acceleration** compared with ICE vehicles. This makes them fun to drive.

Electric vehicles are about **five times more efficient** than ICE vehicles of the same size and weight. This is largely because ICE vehicles turn nearly 80% of the energy of their

2. https://www.harley-davidson.com/us/en/products/bikes/electric-bikes.html
3. https://www.carscoops.com/2021/01/the-story-of-how-and-why-three-wheel-atvs-were-banned/

fuel into heat rather than motion, but electric vehicles produce **very little heat**.[4] Also, all electric cars and some smaller electric vehicles have **regenerative braking**—that is, when you release the accelerator, the car operates the motor in reverse, slowing down the car by using the motor to charge the battery. There is a 3-mile, 7 percent downgrade on the highway near our house. When I drive our plug-in hybrid car down this hill, using the motor to keep the car below 65 mph, the battery has three to four *more* miles available at the bottom of the hill than it had at the top. In contrast, an ICE vehicle uses gas both going up and going down. As a bonus, due to regenerative braking, the brakes on an electric or plug-in hybrid car last many times longer than on an ICE vehicle. A third reason why electric cars are more efficient is that they use almost **no energy while "idling"** at a stoplight. There is very little difference between highway and city mileage for an electric car. In fact, the mileage for city driving is often higher, because you are going at a slower speed, which creates less air resistance.

One disadvantage of electric cars is that the charging infrastructure is still being built out. If you would normally charge the vehicle at home or at work, this is not a problem. But traveling long distance can be a challenge. Also, very cold weather slows down any electro-chemical reaction, including that in electric car batteries. Therefore, if you live in an area that is regularly below freezing in the winter, this is something to consider.

Although electric cars are more expensive to buy than ICE vehicles at present, they are much **less expensive to maintain**. There is no transmission, a very complex and vulnerable part of an ICE vehicle. There is no oil to change,

---

4. https://www.motortrend.com/news/evs-more-efficient-than-internal-combustion-engines/

or spark plugs, or air filters, or cooling system. There is no such thing as a tune-up. You will not have to check the pollution control systems every year or two. There is a slow decrease of battery power, however, and the batteries will at some point need to be replaced, an expensive proposition.

Electric vehicles **benefit the community** as well as the resilient individual. There is **less pollution**, even if some of the energy used comes from fossil fuel-burning power plants. These vehicles are **quieter**, helping the ambiance of the city. On a national level, they **decrease the vulnerability of the country to supply and price shocks** related to the volatile oil market, not to speak of the many ecological problems caused by the process of finding and pumping oil out of the ground.

You can go part-way electric by getting a **hybrid** or a **plug-in hybrid**. Hybrid cars use their electric motor to assist the gasoline engine get moving, using the torque advantage of electric motors. They can also move in reverse and very slowly forward using the electric motor alone, but you cannot drive any distance that way. The battery is charged through regenerative braking, like in pure electric cars. In contrast, plug-in hybrids use only the electric motor to drive the wheels and can go some distance at any speed. The gasoline engine is used only to charge the battery. Thus, both types of hybrids do not have any range problems, like pure electric vehicles.

GET WHAT YOU NEED

The levels below, like the other chapters, are in the order of expense, with the cheapest and easiest steps given first. But unlike other chapters, a higher expense does not necessarily mean a better result for you, society, or the environment. It depends on your needs and your situation. If your transportation needs are satisfied with a bicycle, public transportation, and the occasional rental of a car or the use of Uber or Lyft, then there is no need to move up to the next level, even if you have the resources to do so.

Some bicycles are manufactured in North America, but batteries, electric motors, and their associated controls are often made overseas, which means they could be affected by supply chain issues.

LEVEL 1: WALK AND BICYCLE

Invest in your own transportation and your health at the same time by making an effort to walk or use a bicycle or other human-powered conveyance for as many local trips as possible. My wife and I walk every day, and more than half of the time that walk is do an errand—go to the bank, the pharmacy, the post office, a bookstore, our church, and even a grocery store.

By investing money in a bicycle, and a little of your time and energy, you avoid paying for gasoline and the maintenance on your car, if you have one. If you need to carry some items, invest in a folding two-wheeled cart if you are walking, or a rack behind your bicycle seat and add panniers—they are like saddlebags for a bicycle and attach to both sides of the rack. Or, you can add a basket in front of the handlebars. If you feel unsteady on a two-wheeler or have back issues, invest in a two- or three-wheeled recumbent cycle, which has a backrest and is much closer to the ground. Numerous configurations are now available. As an added benefit to walking and biking, you get exercise (see Chapter 10: Health).

If you decide to use a bicycle regularly for transportation rather than just occasionally for sport, consider a **Dutch-style bicycle**. Remember that the objective in such a bicycle is not speed, but comfort, safety, ease of maintenance, and utility. In contrast to sport bicycles, most Dutch bicycles have:

1. An **upright stance**, as opposed to a horizontal stance. This means that the handlebars are closer to the seat and slightly higher, and they are swept back toward the rider. An upright stance is more comfortable and allows for easier observation of the road and things ahead. Along with this is a **soft saddle**, since nearly your entire weight will be resting on it.

2. **Fenders** front and rear, so that the rider is protected from wet streets after a rain. Many also have a "**skirt guard**" over the upper part of the rear wheel. This is not only to prevent skirts from becoming entangled in the spokes, but also protects the feet of children being carried in a seat on the rack.

3. A **strong rack** in the rear to carry things, or even a passenger, particularly children.

4. No derailleur, but instead has two or three **gears built into the hub**, or only one speed. (The Netherlands is a very flat country.) This keeps the bike simple and not expensive.

5. **Coaster brakes**, rather than caliper or disc brakes.

6. A **key lock** built into the frame, known as a frame lock. It is always available to you, although it only prevents a thief from riding the bike away. He can still carry it off. However, some frame locks now come with a chain as well, so both kinds of protection are available with just one key.

7. A **step-through frame** for easy entry. In the Netherlands, these are not considered to be only for women. This also helps mounting and dismounting the bike when there is a child or a tall package already in the rear seat or rack.

8. A **bell** on the handlebar for warning errant pedestrians or other cyclists.

9. A **full chain guard**, so that your clothes cannot be

soiled by it, and the chain is somewhat protected from the elements.

10. Some kind of **stand** so that the bike can be left upright when not leaning against something.

11. They are made of **steel, not aluminum** or expensive alloys. This and some of the other items make the bike heavier than sport cycles, but again, your objective is comfort and economy rather than speed.

Another step in resilience for your bicycle would be to invest in puncture-resistant tires. They are more expensive than normal tires and are also slightly heavier, but may prevent difficulties down the road.

Savings from this step that can be invested: If you were to walk or bicycle to all local errands, it would be a good savings in gasoline, wear and tear on your vehicle, and possibly fees for parking. If by doing this you were able to avoid the possession of a car altogether, the savings would be very substantial.

LEVEL 2: ELECTRIC BICYCLES

If you live in an area with hills, or it is hot in the summer, walking or biking may be too slow and difficult. In that case, invest in an electric bicycle, or an electric scooter, which has no pedals. Recently some electric bicycles are selling for as little as $900. You can set it to assist your pedaling or push a button to have it carry you without pedaling. If you need to carry more than one child, or a significant amount of things with you, invest in a **cargo bike**, which has an extra-long rack in back of the seat and a very sturdy frame. On the right is an electric cargo bike with both a rack on the back and a basket in the front.[5] I have seen back racks similar to these carrying as many as three small children.

A bakfiets

A variation of the cargo bike is the *bakfiets* (plural *bakfietsen*), invented in the Netherlands. It has a box between the handlebars and the small front wheel that can carry any kind of cargo —groceries, children, pets, etc. The word comes from *bak*, meaning box, and *fiets*, meaning bicycle. It is a brand name, but in popular speech has come to mean any cargo bike of that type. [6]

For even more cargo or children, invest in a **bicycle trailer**. Some are made for carrying small children or pets, and others are made for cargo. The variety of styles and types of electric bicycles available now is amazing—there are ones with fat tires for riding on sand, dirt, or snow; ones that fold for easy storage or taking with you in a car; and some now even have all-wheel drive!

EXAMPLES:

1. The **bicycle messengers** of New York City and other large cities deliver documents and small packages quickly from door to door. Bicycles are nimble and quick to get around and through bad city traffic, and don't have problems with parking.

---

5. Photo by Dan Chabanov of a PakYak E+ bike, https://www.bicycling.com/bikes-gear/a25054215/best-cargo-bikes/
6. https://bakfietscargobikes.com/

2. A person in our neighborhood has an interior **cleaning business**. I often see him riding his bicycle on our street—a large cargo bike with a trailer, both loaded with cleaning supplies.

Bread Bike

3. A local business has recently started in our city called **Bread Bike**. They bake artisan bread and deliver it anywhere in the city with an electric bicycle and a cargo trailer. Delivery services for food and other items also use bicycles.

Savings from this step that can be invested: If the possession of an electric bike enabled you to avoid the purchase of a car, the savings would be substantial.

LEVEL 3: PEDAL ELECTRIC VEHICLES

If you live in an area with significant rainfall, it may be inconvenient to use a bicycle consistently, although the Dutch manage to do it anyway while wearing plastic ponchos, and Finns even use bicycles in the snow. Over a quarter of all journeys in the Netherlands are by bicycle, and they get about 30 inches of rain per year.[7] But if weather is an issue for you, invest in a pedal-electric covered vehicle. These are also known as "bike cars" or "velomobiles." They have three or four wheels, windshields with a wiper, a top, and optional doors as well. They have pedals, and also an electric motor that can either assist your pedaling or power the unit by itself, like an electric bicycle. Some have an

7. https://en.wikipedia.org/wiki/Cycling_in_the_Netherlands

optional solar panel on the top so that the vehicle charges its own batteries. Usually they have headlights, tail lights, and turn signals.

At least three velomobiles are now or will soon be produced in North America—the **ELF**, from North Carolina, the **PEBL**, from Massachusetts, and the **Veemo**, from Vancouver, British Columbia. See Appendix 2 for links and videos. All three cost between $9,000 and $11,000. They have three wheels (two in front, one in the rear), and can carry groceries or a couple of small children in back of the seat. Since these vehicles have pedals and do not travel more than 25 mph or so, they are classified as bicycles, do not require licenses for the vehicle or the operator, and do not require insurance.

In Europe, since gasoline is very expensive, the cities are compact, and it rains often, there are many different models of such vehicles, and more are now in development.

Savings from this step that can be invested: As with the previous level, if the purchase of a velomobile enables you to avoid the purchase of an ICE car, you will have tremendous savings in gasoline, insurance, and other expenses, in spite of the not insignificant expense of purchasing one of these vehicles.

LEVEL 3.5: NEIGHBORHOOD ELECTRIC VEHICLES

Many states allow what are called "Neighborhood Electric Vehicles." Unlike golf carts, these have a fully enclosed cabin like any normal car, and can carry two to four passengers but can only go about 25 or 30 mph and are restricted from traveling on any road with a speed limit over 35 mph (some states 45). They have no provision for carrying golf clubs. These are an excellent way to preserve the mobility of elderly people, while avoiding the risk of serious accidents at high speeds.

An example is the **GEM**, (Global Electric Motors—see Appendix 2), which has been producing these electric vehicles in the U.S. since 1998. GEM vehicles have roofs, headlights, turn signals, and seat belts. Doors are optional. They are often used by companies that have large plants, so the workers can get around quickly, or by large hotels and resorts. They have models with two, four, or six seats, as well as a truck version.

Another example is the **Moke**, which looks like a Jeep with an optional cloth top, no doors, and carries four people.[8]

A "Cadillac" golf cart, complete with Cadillac badges front and rear.

There are also the fancy **golf carts**, many with canvas roofs, that are used by the residents of some large retirement communities, particularly in Arizona. Although they have the fat tires of golf carts, many have probably never been on a golf course! Humorously, some are decked out to resemble mini versions of luxury cars, such as a Cadillac, Mercedes, or Hummer.

An example of a non-retirement area with many vehicles like this is the city of **Avalon** (population 3,700), on Catalina Island off the coast of Los Angeles. The number of motor vehicles allowed on the island is strictly limited and there is no auto ferry. However, they do not count electric "golf"

8. Website: https://mokeamerica.com/

carts as "motor vehicles."[9] Therefore, tourists are taken from the harbor to their hotels on large electric carts, and many of the local residents have them to haul things around, if they are not walking or bicycling. The city of Avalon is very hilly, so having an electric vehicle is useful. Being on a small island, gasoline is also extremely expensive.

Another example is **Peachtree City** in Georgia, population 35,000. The city maintains a network of more than 100 miles of paved roads specifically for electric "golf carts." They are very popular among teenagers, who can use them from age 16 with only a learner's permit. Many teens there drive them to high school, where they have a dedicated parking lot. More than 11,000 carts are registered in the city.[10]

Mackinac Island, Michigan is a resort area that allows no motor transportation at all except for emergency vehicles. Primary means of transportation are walking, bicycles (no electric assist) and horse-drawn carriages, although snowmobiles are allowed in the winter. The permanent population is 583, and the area is 4.35 square miles. Thousands of visitors come in the summer season.[11]

Savings from this step that can be invested: As with the previous level, the savings are substantial if it avoids the purchase of a traditional car. However, you would still need a nearly full-size space to park it, and registration and insurance may be required, depending on your jurisdiction.

---

9. https://www.lovecatalina.com/island-info/plan-your-visit/getting-around/
10. https://www.peachtree-city.org/216/Paths-Golf-Carts
11. https://en.wikipedia.org/wiki/Mackinac_Island

LEVEL 4: ELECTRIC OR PLUG-IN HYBRID CAR AND OTHER ALTERNATIVE FUELS

At the next level up, you invest in an electric car or a plug-in hybrid that can go some number of miles on electric power alone. As with the other levels, if you have solar panels, you are now not only providing your own home electric power, but also your transportation fuel. The Tesla and the Nissan Leaf are the most well known, but nearly every vehicle manufacturer now has electric and/or plug-in hybrid alternatives.

Models are now being designed that have solar panels on the roof which can charge the car when it is sitting in your driveway or you are at work, such as the Lightyear (Dutch company) and the Aptera, a two-seater from California.[12] The first Lightyear model will be very upscale at about $250,000.

Practicality

U.S. Bureau of Transportation Statistics say that the average American drives 29 miles per day.[13] Therefore, a purely electric vehicle is certainly practical for most people most of the time. For those who do occasionally drive long distances, they can either rent a gasoline-powered car or use Lyft or Uber if those occasions are very few, or invest in a plug-in hybrid if those occasions are more often.

New Models Coming

---

12. https://lightyear.one/, https://aptera.us/vehicle/
13. https://www.bts.gov/statistical-products/surveys/national-household-travel-survey-daily-travel-quick-facts

A number of three-wheeled electric cars have entered or are about to enter the market. The advantage of a three-wheeled design is that they are classed as motorcycles, even if they are fully enclosed like a car. Thus, they do not have to adhere to as many regulations, which makes them cheaper. These vehicles carry only two people, usually side by side. Among them are the **Aptera**, which boasts a range of 1,000 miles with the largest battery option, and solar panels on the roof and hood that can add 40 miles per day to the range. Similar to this is the **Nobe**, which has cool retro styling and is based in U.S. but started in Estonia. There are several roadsters, meaning that they have no top: the **Morgan EV3**, the **TORQ Roadster** (400 hp!), and the **Vanderhall Edison 2**. Then there are ones with the two riders in tandem, such as the **Toyota i-Road** (fully enclosed), and the **Arcimoto** (not enclosed).

Three **electric trucks** are already available: the Ford F-150 Lightning, the Rivian and the Tesla "CyberTruck." One or maybe all of them could be game-changers for the transportation industry. At least two electric vans are here or coming soon—the Canoo and a Volkswagen.

On the even larger side, at least one company is soon to launch an **electric motor home**. It will be made by SylvanSport, using a chassis from Zeus Electric, which itself offers many configurations of their 5 ½ ton truck. The range will be about 150 miles.[14]

The Problem with Two-Seaters

There has always been a definite fun factor in two-passenger vehicles since the beginning of motorized transportation. However, it is a niche market, appealing mainly to

---

14. https://www.rvnews.com/sylvansport-developing-all-electric-rv-line/

young single people or empty nesters. My own father had a 1953 Porsche which he brought back from Europe, but it was not practical (and today not even legal) to carry a baby around in such a car with both of the parents, so they soon replaced it with a standard American car with seating for six.

Even today, two-seater cars do not sell well. One of the first hybrid cars was the Honda Insight, a two-seater that was said to get 60 miles per gallon highway or city. It was mechanically sound, but it never sold well, and the second generation Insight is a five-passenger model. The first hybrid car to do well in North America has been the Toyota Prius, a five-passenger sedan. Tesla also entered the market in a big way with the same size vehicle, after first producing a limited number of two-seater sports cars. Therefore, if you buy a two-passenger electric vehicle from a startup company, you will have lots of fun with it, but there is a very good chance that the company, or at least that model will not be here for long.

ALTERNATIVE FUELS

Besides electricity, there are three other transportation fuels that you can theoretically make yourself—biodiesel, alcohol, and hydrogen. But since these are not yet very popular, you will have to be something of a mechanic to utilize them. Therefore, they have been listed as a Level 4 activity.

Biodiesel has been around for a long time. But to make this worthwhile for an individual, you would need access to a free or very cheap supply of used vegetable oil, like from a restaurant that fries food. Before the 1990s, when the possibility of making biodiesel from this oil became general knowledge, restaurants had to pay for someone to haul this used oil away. But then this oil became valuable, and today it is hard to find. In addition, the process of creating biodiesel from this oil takes a significant investment in time and money. Interestingly, the early diesel engines (invented in 1897 by Rudolf Diesel) were often fueled by peanut or sunflower oil, since petroleum was not yet being produced in large quantities.

First, you must filter out the bits of potato, fish, falafel, or whatever has been fried in this oil. You also must also remove any water, which is not difficult because the oil will float above it, so you let the water and any other heavy contaminants out of the bottom of the container through a valve. That is the easy part.

Then you must process the oil to chemically remove the glycerin from the oil. Glycerin makes up about 20% of the oil and makes it too thick to use in a diesel engine, especially when the weather is cold. I have heard about people who install a fuel heater using the engine heat in their diesel vehicle to get around this problem, but this involves having a separate small fuel supply of regular diesel to get your vehicle started and warmed up (and shut it down), and then you switch to the biodiesel.[15] Or, you could come up with your own way to heat the fuel electrically between the tank and the injectors so that it is up to temperature (at least 75 degrees F) before you start the vehicle. Complicated! But it could be worth it if you are not doing short, quick trips. Alternatively, you could blend up to 50% unaltered vegetable oil with petroleum diesel with only a slight drop in energy output.

Removing the glycerin involves heating the oil to between 120 and 130 degrees F, mixing it with potassium or sodium hydroxide (lye) and methanol in precise proportions, and letting it sit for some hours. The glycerin will sink to the

15. https://www.sciencedirect.com/science/article/abs/pii/S0016236113000616

bottom, and the biodiesel will be on top. Let the glycerin out of the bottom of the vessel through a valve. Then you must chemically "wash" the diesel to remove any remaining methanol, because methanol will make the fuel too much like gasoline, and it will also ruin rubber fuel hoses, which are prevalent on diesel vehicles made before 1995.

Then you have to figure out what to do with the glycerin. If you expose it to sunlight for a week, you can make soap, but if you are making significant amounts of biodiesel, you will have a lot of soap! The soap would also smell like whatever was fried in the oil. Since you would not be going through the trouble of making biodiesel if you are making only a small amount, disposing of the glycerin will be an issue.

There are companies that make kits for the production of biodiesel from vegetable oil. One kit makes 43 gallons at a time and costs $2,295.[16] Books are available for $12 which describe how to make your own production kit out of steel drums, pipes, valves, and assorted hardware, if you have mechanical and engineering skills[17]—see the link in Appendix 2 for an overview of the process. You would have to drive for considerable distances and have access to a plenteous and cheap supply of used vegetable oil to make this investment of time and money pay off.

Biodiesel has also been made experimentally using water, algae, air (particularly carbon dioxide), and sunlight. If this process is perfected, it may be possible for individuals to to do it.

---

16. http://udobiodiesel.com/Biodiesel/FuelMeister.html
17. Example: *How to Make Quality Biodiesel at Home: A Simple Step-by-Step Manual & Guide*, Phoenix Xavier, independently published, 2020.

Alcohol: A number of current car models in North America are labeled "flex fuel," which means that they can use a mixture of 85% alcohol and 15% gasoline. In theory, a person could make alcohol at home, if they had a supply of sugary or starchy agricultural produce, some fermentation vats, and a still. Brazil, not having large oil deposits, uses sugar cane to produce much of its transportation fuel in the form of alcohol. The U.S., not having the climate for sugar cane, uses corn to produce alcohol. However, this has the disadvantage of using a food resource to make transportation fuel, a dubious trade-off. Corn is also not as efficient as sugar cane in producing sugar, which means that nearly as much energy is used to produce the fuel as the final result. It is only economic to the motorist because it is subsidized by the federal government.

It would not be any more efficient if a homeowner decided to produce alcohol in this way. However, researchers in Tennessee are experimenting with using switchgrass, a perennial plant that can grow in marginal land not suitable for food crops.[18] If and when they are successful in producing sufficient amounts of alcohol from this grass, it may become an alternative way to produce fuel, particularly for individuals living in rural areas with marginal growing conditions for food crops.

Hydrogen: Using hydrogen as a fuel is a completely different process. First of all, hydrogen can be used in two different ways in a vehicle. It can be **burned in an internal combustion engine** just like natural gas or propane, or it can be used in a **hydrogen fuel cell** to produce electricity that then powers an electric motor. The former method is not

18. https://extension.tennessee.edu/publications/Documents/SP701-A.pdf

being used by anyone commercially at this point because the combustion process makes oxides of nitrogen, a pollutant, due to the nitrogen in the air. It is also only half as efficient as the latter method, which is now being used in several production vehicles made by Toyota, Hyundai, and Honda. The emission of a hydrogen fuel cell vehicle is simply pure water—H2O. Perhaps this water could be collected and used in your garden! However, fuel cells use significant amounts of platinum and iridium, two very expensive metals, which make their widespread use not likely at the present time.

But burning hydrogen in an engine is not out of the running. In early 2023 a British company, JCB Power Systems, claims to have designed an internal combustion engine using hydrogen that avoids the pollution problem. The emission from this engine is only water vapor. They produce construction equipment that operates continuously for eight or more hours a day, for which pure battery power is not practical.[19] Toyota is also working on a hydrogen ICE car.

At the present time, there are a limited number of hydrogen fueling stations, most of which are in California. But for the purpose of investing in your own transportation fuel you could, in theory, build your own hydrogen production apparatus. You would need a supply of pure (distilled or reverse osmosis) water, some chemicals to make the water conduct electricity readily, an apparatus to collect the hydrogen, and a supply of direct current electricity, which splits the water molecules into hydrogen and oxygen. If you have solar panels or a wind turbine, then you already have the direct current electricity. The resulting hydrogen must then

19. https://www.sae.org/news/2023/03/jcb-hydrogen-engine#:~:text=JCB%20unveiled%20their%20clean-sheet%20hydrogen%20combustion%20engine%2C%20the,a%20zero-emissions%20solution%20for%20construction%20and%20agricultural%20equipment.

be pressurized into a canister and transferred into another canister in the vehicle when needed. This technology may become popular in the future. One commercial distribution company in Norway is fueling some medium-distance trucks with hydrogen produced using energy from solar panels on the roof of their building.[20] A Belgian company is also starting to produce solar panels with an integrated system that takes moisture out of the air and makes hydrogen.[21]

Another drawback to the use of hydrogen is the extremely high pressure—at least 5,000 psi, needed to compress it into a liquid form to use conveniently in a vehicle. Having a container with an explosive liquified gas under that amount of pressure located in a vehicle is enough to give an insurance company nightmares. In addition, since hydrogen is the smallest atom, the walls of the container must be thick and specially coated, making them heavy and expensive. However, companies are now working on ways to carry the hydrogen supply in a different, less dangerous form that can be released as the vehicle needs it.

As you can see, there is much to be done to make more alternatives for resilient transportation more available to more people. But an individual, family, or group can do many things even now.

Savings from this step that can be invested: At this level you are providing nearly all your own transportation fuel for local trips, so whatever you are now spending for transportation fuel you can put into savings.

---

20. https://www.oceanhywaycluster.no/news/asko-puts-norways-first-hydrogen-powered-trucks-on-the-road
21. https://www.pv-magazine.com/2022/11/09/hydrogen-producing-rooftop-solar-panels-nearing-commercialization/#:

NEW DEVELOPMENTS TO LOOK FOR:

- New electric cars, motorcycles, and scooters.
- New types of electric vehicle batteries, cheaper, safer and holding more energy than lithium iron phosphate.
- Faster charging speeds and charging stations in more locations.
- Electric RVs, boats, and airplanes
- New ways to make alcohol and diesel fuels from nonfood plants or algae.
- New ways to store hydrogen for use in a fuel cell-powered electric vehicle.
- New, cheaper ways to make hydrogen that do not start with natural gas.
- New internal combustion engines using hydrogen that solve the pollution problem.

CHAPTER 8
SKILLS – BUILD AND FIX IT YOURSELF

He that hath a trade, hath an estate.
Benjamin Franklin

Since we cannot know all that is to
be known of everything, we
ought to know a little about everything.
Blaise Pascal

I have never let my schooling
interfere with my education.
Mark Twain

I like to instruct people. It's noble to
teach oneself. It is still nobler
to teach others, and less trouble.
Mark Twain

We tend to hire experts to aid us with many skills. We assume that many tasks are too complex, so we take the easy and expensive way out and hire someone. We hire experts in many fields—plumbing, electrical, refrigeration and heating systems (HVAC), carpentry, home remodeling, furniture making and repair, appliance repair, woodcarving, metal-working/blacksmithing, masonry, blade sharpening, roofing, tax preparation, buying and selling real estate, medical (first aid and CPR, use of herbs and essential oils, chiropractic, natal and postnatal care), sewing (including knitting and crocheting), hair cutting, styling and braiding, auto maintenance and repair, computer services, landscaping, interior design, graphic design, pottery making, teaching adults or children, childcare, and many others.

You can do many of these things yourself. You can indeed prepare your own taxes, buy or sell your own home, make your own financial investments, and start your own estate plan—I have done all of these things personally at various times. All these services cost a lot to hire. But with a little bit of study, any of us can perform simple tasks in any of these fields. **Let it be like a hobby for you, but one that has very practical uses.**

There are five advantages to this approach. First, you can **tackle the simple tasks in the field you have chosen and save yourself a lot of money**. The key is to be able to recognize a simple task, and distinguish it from one where you might get in over your head and then need a professional to rescue you. If you can distinguish the simple from the complex and then do it, you will be more resilient for a time when a professional is not available.

Second, **knowledge is power**. If you know something about the task at hand, then when you do hire someone to do it professionally, you will know basically what the professional is doing and be able to ask good questions. You will know enough to avoid being taken advantage of, or even avoid a total scam. The classic case is someone taking their car into a shop because of a funny noise or an unknown fluid leak, and being sold a new transmission or other large part when it was not needed. Knowledge adds to your resilience.

The third advantage is **having an alternative occupation**. If you just needed a little extra money, it could be a "side hustle." But if something were to happen so that you could no longer work in your original profession, you would be occupationally more resilient. You would already have an alternative occupation in your back pocket—one that you knew would hold your interest and you already knew something about. You would probably have to do some further training for it and perhaps obtain some kind of license or certification, but you would not be starting from zero.

Fourth, you will have a **useful hobby to engage in after retiring** from your main profession. Many people retire and then don't know what to do with themselves. Some, who have been totally wrapped up in their profession for decades, have their identity so connected with their jobs that they don't have a purpose in life beyond it. A hobby can fill that gap, along with the spiritual pursuits in Chapter 11.

Fifth, after you have learned how to do something, you can **contribute to the resilience of your community** by teaching others. This creates bonds between people, strengthening solidarity with your neighbors and friends as they also become more resilient. In other words, you increase the inter-independence of your community.

There are other skills and hobbies that can be useful or even profitable but may not considered "professions." These include using metal detectors to find coins, rings, and other valuables; "magnet fishing" in lakes or streams with a large magnet on a rope; rock polishing; and knot tying. There are many others too numerous to list.

Don't say "I couldn't do that." Most people can do most tasks—it just depends on your interest in it. These days there are many ways to investigate and learn about a skill or hobby. There are still the traditional ways—books or journals from your library and hanging around a person who already engages in it, like an apprenticeship. Once you are in it, most hobbies have clubs that you can join where you can exchange information, share experiences, and increase your skill.

But today there are also other **ways to learn.** There are YouTube videos on every conceivable hobby or area of expertise. There are websites and articles on the internet. There are internet classes, both free and those that charge a small fee, such as Skillshare, Udemy and Brilliant.org.

There is at least one exception—law. As the saying goes, "He who represents himself in court has a fool for a client."[1] If you are in need of a lawyer to represent you in court, you are most likely in danger of being in deep trouble, and it is no time to wing it on your own. But there could be one exception to this exception: the jailhouse lawyer. In that case, a person may have no other choice but to advocate for himself.

Below is a list of skills that would be personally useful, but could also become a profession. This list is by no means comprehensive. The range is limitless, and is increasing every year as new technologies come on line and need people to operate and interpret them. The key is to see a need and fill it.

SKILLS TO CONSIDER

- **Energy: Electric wiring**
- Fixing appliances, large or small

1. According to quoteinvestigator.com, the earliest version of this adage was written by William de Britaine in 1682. It has been repeated by many writers since then, including some late attributions to Abraham Lincoln.

- Photovoltaic panel system installation
- **Food & Farm: Vegetable and fruit growing**
- Composting
- Greenhouse design and construction
- How to save seeds
- How to preserve food—freezing, drying, canning, fermenting, pasta making
- How to make beer, wine, and distilled spirits
- Animal husbandry, large (cattle, sheep, goats, horses, llamas, etc.)
- Animal husbandry, small (rabbits, poultry)
- Beekeeping
- Foods you can forage in your region
- Fishing in your region
- Hunting and trapping in your region
- Worm farming
- Mushroom growing
- Christmas tree growing
- Dog breeding
- Catering
- Barista
- Extreme couponing
- **Water: Plumbing and sanitation**
- Methods of cleaning and purifying water
- **Construction: Cabinetry**
- House construction
- Furniture making and upholstering
- **Metal working: Pipefitting**
- Sheet metal fabrication
- Welding
- Forging
- Smelting
- **Clothing: Sewing, patching and repairing garments**

- Knitting
- Crocheting
- Tailoring
- Weaving
- **Electronics: Podcasting**
- Website building
- Drone flying and photography
- 3D printing
- Laser cutting and etching
- CAD (computer-aided design)
- **Medical & Health: First aid**
- Basics of midwifery
- Sanitation
- CPR
- Tai Chi, yoga, and other exercise regimens
- Personal trainer
- **Transportation: Changing/fixing a tire on a bicycle, motorcycle, or car**
- Bicycle repair
- Basic motorcycle or auto maintenance and repair
- Small engine maintenance and repair
- Sailing, piloting boats
- Aircraft pilot's license
- Bus or large truck license
- **Communications: Amateur radio ("ham" radio)—short or long range**
- CB and Family Radio Service (FRS)
- Learn a foreign language, including sign language
- **Recreation: Sports—team and individual**
- Chess and other board games
- Skiing—downhill or cross-country
- Snowboarding
- Snowshoeing

- Skateboarding
- Swimming
- Scuba diving
- Lifeguard
- Target and skeet shooting
- Orienteering—finding your way without GPS
- **Artistic and Craft: Drawing and painting**
- Sculpting
- Pottery making
- Basket weaving
- Rock collecting, cutting, polishing & mounting
- Jewelry making
- Henna/temporary tattoos
- Face painting
- Balloon twisting
- Soap making
- Glass blowing
- Candle making
- Calligraphy
- Wood carving
- Storyteller
- Entertainment without the TV or internet
- **Musical: Playing a musical instrument**
- Making musical instruments
- A/V control and remote broadcasting
- Disc jockey
- Singing
- Dancing
- **Personal services: Hospice/elderly care**
- Personal shopper
- Personal assistant—in-person or virtual
- Clean or organize houses
- Recruiter/headhunter
- Mystery shopper/restaurant rater

- Promotional model
- Body part model (e.g., your feet or hands)
- Movie extra
- Lock picking
- Santa/Mrs. Claus
- Character actor at parties
- Work at Renaissance fairs in costume
- Treasure hunt coordinator for events/parties
- Human organ courier
- Dog walker, dog trainer
- Bike messenger/delivery
- Rickshaw operator
- Transcription service
- **Selling: Sell items on line**
- Secondary marketing affiliate
- Join a multi-level marketing organization (but be careful!)
- **Survival skills: Navigation by paper maps, compass, sun and stars**
- How to build, start and maintain a fire with various materials and conditions
- Ancient skills such as making spears, arrows, bows, animal traps, etc.
- Purifying water (there are many ways!)
- Knot tying
- Survival in very hot or cold weather
- Signaling for help
- Self-defense—martial arts
- Security

In a similar vein, high school students should be learning some basic useful skills beyond reading, writing, and mathematics. Among these should be how to fill out a simple income tax form, cooking (for boys as well as girls), the basics about insurance, basic home repair, self-defense, survival skills appropriate to the local geography and climate, social etiquette, personal finance, public speaking, basic car maintenance, and stress management. Some young people may already be very skilled in one of more of these areas, but all of them should know the basics in order to thrive when they leave home.

LEVEL 1: DEVELOP ONE EXPERTISE

Besides your existing expertise in your chosen profession, pick up at least one skill that is basic to living, from those listed above, or is related to one of the other chapters in this book, such as gardening or water systems, or is a need in your community. Find a friend, neighbor, or co-worker with the same interest and ask questions. Take the steps mentioned above to collect information. Start with simple tasks in this area that you need to have done and work your way up.

For example, I wanted to increase the ventilation in my attic. So, I investigated making some vents in the soffit area of my roof. Since this is under the eaves, I felt confident to do this myself, since I would not be creating any danger of a roof leak. But then I found out that there was no connection between the soffit area and the rest of the attic, so a vent there would not help. A new vent would have to be on top of the roof and involve a hole in the roof. That's a step beyond what I'm comfortable with, so a professional was needed.

Or, you might have an interest in cooking, though you have never done anything past putting a prepared dinner in the microwave. Find a friend who has similar taste in food. If you are vegan, find another vegan. If you like meat, find another carnivore. Ask them to help you to get started. Then, look up online something you would like to eat and follow the recipe. Once you have prepared a few meals from scratch in this way, you will start to think of ways you could customize these meals for your own tastes.

These days the new cars are very complex, but it is always helpful to **know a few basic things about your car**. Learn the difference between fuel, radiator fluid, engine oil, and transmission fluid. Learn what to do if your car overheats, and how to diagnose the possible reasons why. Find out the reasons which are relatively simple to fix, and which ones might mean your car is toast. If your car won't start, learn what simple things you can check. Learn which basic tools and equipment you should have in your garage or home, and which ones you should have in the car at all times. Make a list of the parts of your car you should check before making a long trip out of town. Learn how to change the oil and the windshield wipers, and how to fill up the windshield wiper fluid tank. Know what kinds of fluid could or should be put into that tank, and whether those fluids differ with the season. Even with the complexity of today's vehicles, it is possible to know how to do all of the above yourself. Knowing these things will make you more resilient regarding your transportation, and could also save you lots of money.

If you have children, urge them also to develop more than just one interest. Follow this formula: Show them how to do something, watch them while they do it, then let them do it on their own. Let them explore many options. For example, when my son was young, we could see and hear that he had an ear for music, so I got him a guitar and taught him a few chords, and we made sure we had a simple synthesizer at home. . Later we got him lessons in both the guitar and piano. Today he plays guitar much better than I ever did. He never made a career out of it, but if he wanted or needed to do it, he could.

If someone you know is majoring in one subject in college, urge them to minor in something very different—perhaps something that they are already taking classes in. The intersection of two subjects is where you can easily become an expert in high demand. For example, the intersection between nursing and IT is a growing field, because of the increased digitization of medical records. Accounting added to any other field can make you a key person. If you know farming and business, you are invaluable.

Savings from this step that can be invested: Depending on what kind of skill you choose, the savings could be minor or very significant.

LEVEL 2: DEVELOP SEVERAL ABILITIES

Now pick up a second skill in an area unrelated to the first. If your first extra skill is something mechanical like carpentry or plumbing, choose something very different, like cooking or a medical-related skill.

Continue to develop your first expertise by joining a club or group that engages in that activity. The members will probably help each other with tips and hacks, and you will develop your knowledge and abilities.

Savings from this step which can be invested: Your savings here would add to the savings from Level 1.

LEVEL 3: TRADE OR SELL YOUR SERVICES, TEACH OTHERS

Trade or barter your service with others, where legal. For example, you unplug your neighbor's toilet, and she mends your jacket. Or you help her preserve some backyard fruit, and she gives you advice on your garden. This is inter-independence in action.

You can also sell your services, when and where legal. You may need to become certified, or obtain a license do this. In addition, now that you have one or more areas of expertise, you can teach others, either singly or in groups. See Appendix 2 for a list of possible places to do this.

Bonus: You can have the job done your way—customized for your needs.

Bonus #2: Even professionals can be out of date and may not know things. Do your own research, and you will be way ahead.

Savings from this step that can be invested: The savings at this level go up substantially because you are trading or selling your skill, as well as using it in your own life.

NEW DEVELOPMENTS TO WATCH FOR:

- New websites that can teach you how to do things.

- New clubs or organizations in your community that can sharpen your skills, teach you new ones, or give you a venue to teach others.
- New online marketplaces where you can sell your services.

CHAPTER 9
FINANCIAL RESILIENCE

Divide your portion to seven, or even to eight, for you do not know what misfortune may occur on the earth.
Ecclesiastes 11:2

There are three faithful friends— an old wife, an old dog, and ready money.
Benjamin Franklin

Financial resilience is based on the same principle as other areas of resilience—the fact that **unexpected events happen** from time to time. Many of these unexpected events are financial in nature. **Financial panics** are numerous throughout history, the latest being the Great Recession of 2008, caused by a bubble in the housing market and the proliferation of housing loans to unqualified buyers. **Hyper-inflation** has devastated many countries, including Germany after the First World War (up to 30,000% per month), Hungary in 1946 (42 quadrillion percent per month—prices doubled every 15 hours), Argentina in the 1980s and 90s (up to 20,000% per month), and Zimbabwe from 2007-2009 (up to 489 billion percent per month). Paradoxically, **deflation** is also a financial disaster, particularly for anyone who has borrowed money and has to pay it back in money that is more valuable. Japan experienced this during the 1990s.

Many other kinds of **unexpected non-financial events can directly affect your finances**—you could lose your job, your business, or an investment you made fails. And if something happens to an area of life that is not specifically financial—your house, your food or water supply, your health, or the health of a loved one—they will all affect your financial situation one way or another. Those who are financially resilient will certainly be impacted by these kinds of events, but they will not be devastated.

On top of these personal reasons to become financially resilient, you will also **help your community**. When (not *if*!) a disaster strikes, you will be in a position to help your relatives, friends, and neighbors financially. In addition, when you model financial resilience, the young people in your life will be watching, and you hope they will follow your example. I am not a businessman, but both of our children have been wise in their financial dealings. When our daughter was growing up she observed how our family prepared for potential adversities and shortages when we lived in Central Asia. Therefore she was much more prepared than many of her friends when the COVID-19 pandemic struck in early 2020.

There are **five important ways to be financially resilient:** have an emergency fund, properly cover yourself with insurance, be legally up to date, avoid debt, and be diversified.

1. Emergency Fund: The first and most important way to be financially resilient is to have the ability to weather financial adversity—being laid off from your job, an illness of yourself or someone in your family, a natural disaster, or a general economic downturn or even meltdown. In 2015 the Pew Charitable Trusts discovered that a household has a 60 percent chance of some kind of unexpected expense every year.[1] Thus, you must have an emergency fund—a stash of money in a safe place that will sustain you when an unexpected expense comes your way. Unfortunately, statistics from the Federal Reserve showed that in late 2021, 32 percent of Americans could not cover a $400 emergency expense with cash or its equivalent.[2] The personal financial guru Suzi Orman said in November 2023 that "...75% of the people in the U.S. don't have $400 to their name in case of an emergency."[3] The large discrepancy between these figures could be due to the fact that during the pandemic, people could not spend money on restaurant meals, travel, and other luxuries while they received stimulus checks from the government. But as soon as the pandemic ended, as Suzi Orman explained, spending went up, income went down, and savings disappeared.

Ideally, you will have enough in this fund to sustain you for six to nine months without the income from your job. This means having enough money to pay for basic things—mortgage and property taxes or rent, utilities, food, insurance, and transportation. Include about half of what you now spend per month for eating out and other entertainment, and

---

1. AARP Bulletin January/February 2021, p. 18
2. https://www.fool.com/the-ascent/personal-finance/articles/the-number-of-americans-able-to-cover-a-400-emergency-reaches-a-9-year-high/#:~:text=In%20a%20May%202022%20report%20based%20on%20data,%24400%20emergency%20expense%20using%20-cash%20or%20its%20equivalent.
3. 'The government's not going to save them': Suze Orman warned of a looming financial 'pandemic' — says Americans have no one to rely on. Here's what she means and how to prepare (msn.com)

do not include any major purchases. Thus this amount would generally be a bit less than you now spend in a typical six to nine months. If you had such a fund, then you would be able to survive through a layoff, being fired, or other employment calamity. If you are self-employed, you could survive a downturn in your business that happened through an unforeseen event such as a pandemic.

Insurance protects us against many forms of calamity, but nevertheless, there are always **things that are not covered** by insurance. The Pew Charitable Trust said in 2015 that households have a 60 percent chance of some type of unexpected expense every year, the median cost of which was $2,000. Some have said that you ought to have money available equal to your largest insurance deductible, or perhaps all of your deductibles added together.

Having an emergency fund saved up is certainly a form of resilience all by itself. But it is also an investment, assuming this money is in the bank and not under your mattress. These days, money in the bank pays very little, but there may come a time when it will pay something significant.

2. Insurance: The basic principle of insurance is to cover you for a loss that would be very bad for you, or even catastrophic. For example, getting cancer is a catastrophic event. Treatment costs hundreds of thousands of dollars, if not millions. Insurance against such an event is extremely important.

On the other hand, the loss of a 20-year-old car in poor condition would not be catastrophic for many people, so it would be a waste of money to buy insurance for it. If you had a car like that, buy only liability insurance, which covers damage to the other person's car if the accident is your fault.

Aside from legal requirements, it is possible that the other person in an accident caused by you could have a Lamborghini, and you would be on the hook for lots of money!

Most insurance policies have **deductibles**. The attitude of many people is that the lower the deductible, the better, and having no deductible at all is the best situation. Not so! When you have no deductible, you are paying the insurance company to process all of your low-value claims. This is expensive for them, and they charge you a lot of money to do that. It would be better to **pay the low value claims yourself**, out of your emergency fund. Then your insurance will be much cheaper, and you can use the money you save to put more money into your emergency fund and get an even higher deductible the next time. You can see how this will snowball to your advantage.

Instead of paying for low deductibles, **buy high limits** per occurrence, and per year. For example, on your auto insurance, the difference in premium between a $300,000 limit on claims and a $1 million limit on claims is very small. Buy it! The chance of a claim exceeding $300,000 is very small, which is why the premium for this extra protection is low. But if, God forbid, something like that would happen, it could ruin you. This is precisely the situation for which insurance was created.

3. Be Legally Up To Date: Make sure that the named **beneficiaries** on all your accounts are up to date. Also, everyone must **have a will**. This avoids most problems between your heirs after you die, and could also save your estate lots of money. If your estate is over several million dollars, then you probably should have a Living Trust, which will save your heirs lots of hassle and money. In addition, **check your Social Security statement** to make sure that you are being credited properly. Mistakes can happen, and scammers can even claim your benefits if they somehow get your Social Security number!

4. Avoid Debt: The fourth way to be financially resilient is not to be in debt. A debt is an unchangeable item in your monthly budget, in most cases, unless you were to declare bankruptcy. The debt doesn't care if you lose your job, fall sick and can't work, or face some other financial difficulty. Having debt is a sign of not being resilient. As King Solomon said long ago, "the borrower is the slave of the lender" (Proverbs 22:7). He said this because it is a description of the way the world *is*, not the way it *should* be.

Some debts are worse than others. Debts with high interest rates are worse than those with low interest rates. A debt on an asset that rises in value, such as a home, is much less of a problem than a debt for an item that falls in value, such as a car.

Avoid student debt, which is how many people become burdened with debt in the first place. In 2018, the average college graduate had about $29,000 in student debt. About 25% of graduates owe between $40,000 and $80,000, and 10% owe more than that. Huge student debts are causing many young people to avoid marriage or having children, preventing them from being able to buy a house, and constraining their career choices to those where they must make a lot of money to pay back the debt. Their lives are not resilient!

Each person should give serious thought to ways in which college debt can be avoided. If you are in high school, try to **pass as many college-level classes as possible during high school**, for starters. This could save as much as a whole semester of time and tuition. Secondly, **community colleges** are much less costly, so one's college education can start there. To continue, state universities are usually much less expensive than private ones. However, investigate the situation carefully. The course of study our daughter pursued would have taken eight years at a state university, due to overcrowded classes in that major (nursing) at that time, but it took her only four and a half years at a private university. Investigate all possible sources for discounts and scholarships. Sometimes, a private university can be cheaper than a state university if they give a lot of scholarship help.

Once you are in the job market, employers generally do not care which university granted your diploma. Famous ivy league universities teach basically the same information as all other universities, but at many times the cost. The only possible benefit to elite universities is the opportunity to make friends with high-achieving people (classmates) that will serve as your networking base when you begin your career, if your career is the type that would benefit from such networking, like law, business, or politics.

Work Colleges: There are also at least eight private colleges in the United States that cost absolutely nothing. All the students must work their way through at jobs provided by the college. See Appendix 2 for a website that lists them. In addition, there are also technical colleges, some of which also charge no tuition for the same reason.

Military Service is another option to avoid student debt. This can be done two ways: by attending one of the service academies (West Point, Annapolis, Air Force Academy, Coast Guard Academy), or by serving first and then attending a university of your choice through the GI Bill.

If you're considering college or a career change, ask yourself, **do I really need a college degree?** Seriously consider whether the profession you want to enter really requires a four-year degree at all, or whether self-study combined with an apprenticeship or other mentoring would do as well. Many careers in the high-tech area require or value relevant experience, higher than a diploma. Companies like Google and Apple are going this route.[4] Consider that Mark Zuckerberg, the founder and head of Facebook, did not finish his course at Harvard University, and yet has been very successful.

Also consider your own interests in academic work. Most colleges and universities in North America require courses in a wide range of subjects that may not interest you at all, such as English, mathematics, history, social studies, and other liberal arts. Why torture yourself in these classes and rack up lots of debt for the privilege if this is not your interest?

Finally, consider taking a **gap year**—a year after you finish high school, in which you take a job or, if you have money, do some travel, or perhaps both. This year can help you to clarify what you would like to do with your life, so that you do not waste time and money on a course of study that you later find was not your thing.

As for **other debts**, one should **avoid borrowing money to buy a depreciating asset**. Nearly everything you can buy depreciates except for real estate, so borrowing to buy your house is OK, but avoid all other debts. Another reason to avoid other debt is the fact that real estate loans have the lowest interest rates, and all other loans have higher rates. Therefore, avoid borrowing money to buy a car. Instead, buy a used car—one that is several years old, but doesn't have

---

4. https://www.cnbc.com/2018/08/16/15-companies-that-no-longer-require-employees-to-have-a-college-degree.html#:~:text=Job-search%20site%20Glassdoor%20compiled%20a%20list%20of%20-top,Apple%20and%20IBM%20are%20all%20in%20this%20group.

too many miles on it. Better yet, use other methods of transportation discussed in Chapter 7 if you can, or take public transportation until such time as you can pay cash for your car, if you truly need one.

Finally, **never take on debt for someone else**. In other words, never co-sign for a loan for anyone, even a friend or relative. When you do that, it is very possible that their debt will become your debt. If someone cannot get a loan without a co-signer, this is a sign that this is a risky proposition that you should not get involved with. According to a survey published in 2019, 60 percent of Americans have lent money to a friend or relative, including 21 percent who have co-signed on a financial product.[5] Of the total number of people, 35 percent have either lost money, had their credit score damaged, or harmed their relationship with that friend or relative. Co-signing has a good chance of decreasing your financial and social resilience.

Related to this, **avoid lending money to friends or relatives**. Loaning money to them is a good way to ruin your relationship with that person. They will feel indebted to you and will likely be embarrassed and avoid seeing you if they are having trouble paying you back. If you really desire to help the person, and you know that this money will not be used to enable them to continue bad behavior, then **give them the money as a gift**, so that you assume in your own mind that this money is gone and will not be returned. Obviously, in this case, it must be money that you are absolutely positive you will not need in the future. If this person later gets their life back on track, they can "gift" you the money

---

5. https://www.bankrate.com/finance/credit-cards/lending-money-survey-2019/#:~:text=According%20to%20the%20survey%2C%2021%20percent%20of%20Americans,harmed%20and%2020%20percent%20damaged%20their%20credit%20scores.

(or an item of value) back. Your relationship is preserved no matter what the outcome.

5. Diversify: The fifth way to be financially resilient is to diversify—never have all your financial eggs in one basket. I would agree with the quote at the beginning of the chapter from Ecclesiastes (King Solomon lived nearly 3,000 years ago!) that for an individual investor, seven or eight is a good number of "baskets" for diversification. Any less, and you are not diversified enough. More than eight major areas of investment become very difficult for an individual person to monitor with any consistency.

The wisest course is to diversify in several ways, to cover as many possible situations as you can. First, **diversify the level of risk**. A bank account is considered very safe, since in the U.S. they are protected by the Federal Deposit Insurance Corporation up to $250,000. At the other end of the spectrum, there are investments in commodities and stock options where you can lose your entire investment in only a few hours if the market suddenly changes. Stocks and bonds are somewhere in the middle and vary from somewhat safe to rather risky. If a company goes bankrupt, you may lose the whole thing. My father bought some junk bonds that paid 18% interest in the 1980s. This was a great investment, until Pan American Airways went bankrupt in 1991 and the investment became a total loss other than the interest that had already been paid.

You also must **diversify your type of investments**. Do not have only stock, or only bonds, or only real estate, or only bank deposits, safe as some of these might appear to be on the surface.

LEVEL 1: BEGIN YOUR EMERGENCY FUND, LEGAL UPDATE, INSURANCE

Begin Your Emergency Fund: The initial amount you shoot for depends on how much you can save each month and what your monthly expenses are. Try to have at least $100 in cash available at home, and $300 available in a savings account at your bank. Put the cash somewhere safe in your house, but not where you put your everyday money. Have it in $20 bills, not in $100 bills that might be hard to spend when you need it. Do not put the bank money in your checking account, or you might be tempted to spend it. Instead, establish a separate savings account for it.

Legal Update: While you are at the bank, **check the beneficiaries** of all your accounts. Your life situation may have changed since you established them, and it would be a mess if you were to die and these papers did not represent reality today. Perhaps you got married or divorced, or you added a child to your family. Also, **make a will** if you do not have one already. If your estate is not large or complex, then the will does not have to be fancy—you can find examples online for free or very cheaply. Make sure that a witness also signs it, and you have at least two copies stored in different locations. Also, be sure that someone other than you and your spouse knows where it is. If someone dies without a will, then a court has to decide what happens to your possessions.

Insurance: Make sure you are covered by **health insurance**. The lack of health insurance can lead to financial ruin—the very opposite of resilience. These days, with the emphasis on this area, there are low-cost programs to cover you in every state. If you have dependents, buy **life insurance**. When you are young, life insurance is cheap, and in the unlikely event that your dependents need it, they will certainly benefit. If you own a house you should have **fire insurance**, whether you have a mortgage or not. Make sure that it covers "replacement value" rather than "market value." If you live in an area subject to **floods** or **earthquakes**, make sure you have coverage for those events so you can be resilient in the event of a disaster. These last two calamities are not generally covered by fire insurance, so you must check your policy. If you are in a zone that is marked as a "100- or 500-year flood" zone, do not assume you are OK. These maps are notoriously inaccurate, and the weather is more extreme today than in decades past. If there is any kind of creek or river in your vicinity and you are not way uphill from it, assume that it can flood, and cover your risk with insurance.

Savings from this step that can be invested: Having an emergency fund will enable you to avoid payday lenders, racking up credit card debt, imposing on friends or relatives, or dipping into your retirement funds. The first two cost big time. Proper insurance could allow you to avoid a financial catastrophe.

LEVEL 2: INCREASED EMERGENCY FUND, BEGIN FREEING YOURSELF FROM DEBT

Emergency Fund: As soon as you can, increase your emergency fund to $300 in cash at home, and $3,000-$5,000 in an account at your bank. Have this money in an account that pays interest. In recent years, the interest paid on such an account is near zero, but in normal times, this interest will add up, especially if the money is left there for years, which you hope it will be. If possible, automate your savings by having your bank automatically take just a little money from your paycheck and put it in the savings account where your emergency fund is each paycheck, until it is up to the amount that is your goal. Banks are very happy to do that for you!

If you find that it is difficult for you to save money due to the credit card burning a hole in your pocket, then you may need to take a radical step. Cut up your credit cards and replace them with debit cards.

Free Yourself from Debt: First, **check your credit score**, if you don't know it already. This will give you a baseline—a starting point. Check it regularly—every month or so, particularly if you have a number of debts and credit cards. If someone has stolen your identity, this is one way that you will find out.

There are **two strategies to get rid of debt**. The first is popularly known as the **"snowball method."** Write down all your debts, from the smallest to the largest. Start paying them off, starting with the smallest, which will take only a short time. The advantage of this method is that you will have a psychological advantage of rather quick results at the beginning, when it is the most difficult to get started.

The second method is known as the **"avalanche strategy."** Write down your debts in order from the highest interest rate to the lowest, and pay them off in that order. Financially, this strategy is the best in most cases because the higher interest rates are hurting you the most. Using either strategy, your home loan will be the last debt to be paid because it is usually the largest amount and also probably carries the lowest interest rate. Also, as noted above, your home likely is going up in value, so a loan on that kind of asset is not as bad for your resilience.

Do not take your eyes off the prize of financial resilience. If you are tempted to buy something, refocus on your goal. It will take some discipline. It is essential that your spouse or partner be with you in this goal.

Savings from this step that can be invested: Even when interest rates are low, debt is expensive. When the rates go up, debt can be devastating, so the savings for not having debt can be substantial. Invest those savings by reducing your debt even more!

LEVEL 3: FULL EMERGENCY FUND, REDUCE DEBTS TO HOME ONLY, SPECIAL SAVINGS FUNDS, BEGIN INVESTING, GIVE BACK

Full Emergency Fund: Here is where you complete your emergency fund to a full **six to nine months of ordinary expenses** and have it socked away in a safe account at a bank earning interest. You have about $1,000 of it in actual cash in a safe place at your house. Do not have this money in $100 bills, which are hard to spend anywhere, but mostly 20s and 50s.

Pay Off Your Mortgage: In this level, you also finish paying off all of your credit cards and other debts and have only your mortgage. Once you get to that point, begin to pay that off early as well.

To pay off your mortgage as fast as possible, one technique is to pay half of your payment twice a month, instead of one payment once a month—this is called bimonthly payments. For example, instead of paying $1,000 one time a month, pay $500 at the regular payment time, and $500 half a month earlier. You are still paying the same amount every month, but half of the amount is two weeks early. Check with your lender if you can do this. It will save you a considerable amount of money over the long term.

Another way is instead of making one monthly payment, make payments every two weeks. This is called biweekly payments and is similar to the previous idea, but over the course of a year, you would be making 26 payments instead of 24 (13 full-month payments instead of 12). Naturally, making more payments in a year allows you to pay off your debt faster. Again, you would have to check with your lender if this is an option for you according to the contract.

Or, if you can simply make payments early, do it. If someone asks why you would do such a thing, ask them where they can make an investment that will pay them 5% guaranteed (or whatever the rate of your mortgage is). In any case, strive to have your mortgage paid off before you retire so that you are free from that burden.

Invest Your Savings: Since you are no longer paying for lots of debt, you will have a lot more money every month. Don't spend it! Instead, invest it, so that you will be even better off later. The average American saved only 8.83 percent of their income in 2019, a paltry amount compared to East Asian countries, where people save over 35%.[6] In 2020 during the pandemic, the American savings rate

6. https://www.statista.com/statistics/246234/personal-savings-rate-in-the-united-states/#:~:text=The%20statistic%20presents%20the%20average%20personal%20saving%20rate,to%20save%20a%203.3%20percent%20of%20their%20income., https://www.economist.com/finance-and-

increased to over 16 percent, probably due to the fact that many stores were closed, the federal government distributed pandemic aid, and people were panicked into saving. But in 2022, the American savings rate plummeted back down to 3.3 percent.

Invest in some of the **items that will build your resilience**, mentioned in the earlier chapters. Invest in energy-efficient light bulbs, a garden to grow your own fruit and vegetables, rain barrels to collect water for your garden, a food dehydrator to preserve your harvest, and eventually an electric bicycle or car and solar panels to charge them with your own electricity.

Special Financial Investment Options: The first place you should invest your extra funds is in your own retirement. Social Security will not sustain you by itself—ask anyone in that position now and they will tell you. First, maximize your contribution to your company's **401(k)** program. If your company matches your contribution, then for sure contribute at least that amount. That's free money!

You can also establish an Individual Retirement Account (**IRA**). Remember that these are for individuals, so your spouse should also establish their own account. Put the maximum amount into this account every year. Even if you are in your 20s, start it now. There are two kinds of IRAs. The **"traditional" IRA** is funded with "pre-tax money." That is, whatever you put into this fund is not subject to income tax. But when you take the money out, during your retirement, it is taxed. The theory is that you will not be working at that time, and therefore you will be making less

economics/2019/11/21/excess-asian-savings-are-weighing-on-global-inter est-rates money, and be in a lower tax bracket. The **Roth IRA** (named after Senator Roth, who came up with this idea) is funded with money that has already been subject to income tax. When you take the money out of this fund during your retirement, it is tax-free. This if for people who think they might be taking in more money during their retirement years than they are now. You must figure out which kind of IRA would be best for your situation, as best you can foresee the future.

The next place to invest is in a **Health Savings Plan** (HSA) if you are not yet retired. This is an account which can grow tax-free, and out of which you can pay for any medical expenses, such as deductibles, co-pays, and any other medical items not covered by insurance. Usually, the account will issue you a debit card, which makes it easy to pay these items. You can consider this a part of your emergency fund.

A final place to invest is a **529 College Savings Plan**, if you have children. Each state has its own plan(s), which can be used to pay tuition, fees, and room and board at any educational establishment. You can direct where your fund is invested, from a list of mutual funds, ETFs (exchange-traded funds), bank products, and other similar choices.

If you know for sure where your child will attend for university, there are also prepaid tuition plans, but these are limited to tuition only, and not other expenses. Also, who can know, years ahead of time, where their child will want to attend, or even be able to attend?

Diversify: Then you are ready for some personal financial investments. The operative word here is diversify, as King Solomon advised. You will want diversity of risk, diversity of economic sector, diversity of type of investment, and finally diversity between liquid and non-liquid investments.

Diversity is your protection because in spite of what some people claim, **no one can predict what will happen to the market** in the short term, meaning less than three years. You will find many books or websites that will claim to tell you some system of picking stocks and other investments—"charting" (predicting on the basis of what the price chart has looked like for some period of time up to the present), various kinds of waves or repeating patterns, psychological factors, and others. The truth is, there are so many factors at work that you would have to know every fact about almost everything in the world in order to know where the market was going to move next week, let alone next month or year. Even then you would not really know, because psychological factors are at work in the market that no one can know.

Therefore, it is **foolish to try to "beat the market,"** and even more foolish to pay someone else to try to beat the market with your money. Statistically, there will always be those who beat the market for a year or even several years, but given enough time, their results will approach average. The best thing you can do is diversify.

One historical exception to not being able to predict the future of the market was portrayed in the book *The Big Short* by Michael Lewis and later made into a film. In this famous real incident in 2008, one financial analyst named Michael Burry figured out that most home loan collateralized debt obligations (a type of bond consisting of a bundle of other debt instruments) consisted of very risky (subprime) home loans, most of which were in danger of defaulting. If a number of them started defaulting, it would create a snowball effect that would crash the real estate market and cause most of the other loans to default, thus reducing the value of these bonds to near zero. Burry and a few of his friends borrowed lots of money and took financial positions against these bonds, and made literally billions of dollars in less than a year.

In this case, one very smart and skilled financial analyst spent a long time (weeks, working night and day) to figure this out. There are times and places where this level of investment of time could yield enough information that is not known by the general public so that you could beat the market for a short time. But these times and places are rare. Usually, by the time you have figured out a system to beat the market, others have also figured it out (or soon will) and the benefit is lost. It is much more profitable for the average person in most cases to diversify risk.

A **bank savings account** is the prime example of a very low level of risk. They are insured by an agency of the federal government, so unless the entire government and financial system goes down, you are covered. And if the whole government went down, finding out what happened to your money would be the least of your worries! On the other end of the spectrum would be stock options or commodities like wheat or oil. If you made the wrong call on one of these, you could lose your entire investment in only a few days or even a few hours. Many supposedly smart people lost millions in January 2021 by buying options on Game Stop stock, which went up instead of down as they expected.[7]

When you are young, you can have a majority of your investments in somewhat risky investments like a stock fund. When you are retired, you want less of your money in the more risky investments because you don't have as much time to wait while they come back after a downturn.

You also want **diversity of economic sector**. Do not put all your money into a high-tech stock fund, even if you are sure that high tech is going to be huge in the next five years.

---

7. https://en.wikipedia.org/wiki/GameStop_short_squeeze

If you work for a company that gives you their stock as part of your compensation or your 401(k), do not leave the majority of your investment in that one stock. Diversify! You can invest in utilities, consumer goods, mining, or foreign companies.

Types of financial investments available to the average person include stocks, bonds, and real estate. Stocks are the most volatile—they can go up and down quickly. Bonds usually move more slowly, and usually in the opposite direction of stocks. When people think that stocks will not go up further, they sell stock and buy bonds, causing them to rise, and making the interest rate they pay go down. This is because a bond, once issued, pays a fixed dollar amount every six months. If you pay more for that bond, the interest rate to you, the purchaser, is less.

Real estate also comes in several forms—residential, commercial, farm land, and raw land. Raw, undeveloped land will not give you any dividend—it is pure speculation, unless you are going to use it for something yourself. Commercial property can go up and down with your local business climate. It is somewhat more risky than residential property, because unless people are homeless, everyone must live somewhere. A commercial property can be vacant for a long time, but at some price, a residential property will nearly always be occupied. Another more diversified way to invest in real estate is through a **Real Estate Investment Trust** (REIT). These are bought and sold like stocks—you buy a share of a REIT on the stock exchange, and they pay dividends like stocks.

The easiest way to diversify your stock or bond investments is with a **mutual fund** or an **exchange-traded fund** (ETF). A mutual fund is a company that invests your money in a range of companies, and pays you a dividend based on their average profit. Some will charge you a fee up front

(front load), and other will charge you a fee only if you cash out before a period of time, like five years (back load). Others are “no-load” funds. All funds charge an administration fee, and you have to watch that, because it will eat into your gains. A difference of only 0.75% per year, after 20 years, will result in 20% less money in your account!

An **ETF** is a closed-end fund—you can’t just buy your way in. You have to buy a share of the fund from someone else who is selling it, and they are sold on the stock market just like General Electric or Apple stock. The fund is invested in whatever sector of the market that is their specialty, and they pay dividends. The biggest difference from a regular mutual fund is that the share price goes up and down, just like any other stock. You can buy an ETF that mimics the broad market, like the Standard & Poor’s 500 index (S&P 500). This would be the best place for someone starting to invest. There are ETFs for both stocks and bonds.

The downside of investing in mutual funds or ETFs is that you have no control over what kind of companies that they will invest in. If you would rather that your money not be invested in oil companies, or companies that make alcoholic drinks, or tobacco products, or guns, or some other particular item, it may be difficult to find a fund that fits that desire. You may be able to find a socially responsible fund (also known as ESG—environmental, social and corporate governance investing) that fits your ethics, but perhaps not.

A final type of diversity is **liquid and non-liquid** investments. A liquid investment is one that you can “cash out” easily and with little or no penalty. You can take your money out of a passbook saving account or a money market account at any time with no notice and without charge. You can sell a stock, bond, mutual fund, or ETF at any time and just pay a small brokerage fee—these days it is often only $5 or less. Examples of non-liquid investments would be a business venture or real estate. The investments in the earlier chapters of this book are also non-liquid because it would be difficult to sell them.

It is best, and maximizes your resilience, if you are diversified in as many of the dimensions as possible. When you start out investing, you will not be very diversified, but as you accumulate more capital, you can diversify more and more. To start, at Level 3, put money in one or two mutual funds or ETFs, such as a fund that mimics the S&P 500, and a bond fund.

Give Back to Your Community: You should always be giving back to your community, no matter what your financial condition. If you are "in the hole" financially, much of that giving back might be in the form of time rather than money. But once you have climbed out of the hole, consider giving substantially to your community, so that others can be put on the road to resilience. Increase the inter-independence of your community! See Appendix 2 under Chapter 9 for some ideas of worthy organizations.

In general, you will want the organization you are helping not only to be financially honest but also to be working on the root causes of problems in your community, rather than just treating the symptoms. The organization should follow the adage that if you give a man a fish, you feed him for a day, but if you teach him to fish, you feed him for a lifetime.

Savings from this step that can be invested: Your main savings from this step will be not paying for other people to manage your money because you are capable of doing it yourself. Take the money that you would have been paying to them and invest it.

LEVEL 4: NO DEBT, RETIREMENT SET, FULLY DIVERSIFIED, PICK YOUR OWN INVESTMENTS

No Debt, Retirement fully funded: At this level you have paid off all your debt, fully funded your 401(k) and your IRA, and have invested a significant amount in a diverse selection of mutual funds—both stocks and bonds.

Pick Your Own Investments: Now you can think about getting rid of the management fees charged by mutual funds and ETFs and doing your own diversification with the stock portion. This will allow you to keep that money for yourself.

If you are invested in stocks or bonds, **diversify** also in the industries that these stocks represent. Do not put all your stock investments in pharmaceutical stocks, for example, even if they are "hot" at the time. Something may happen to the pharmaceutical industry as a whole, and then all your stocks would fall at the same time.

To make these decisions, people often rely on financial services professionals, whether they are associated with your bank, a brokerage firm, or an independent company. If you don't educate yourself about the financial world, then you are dependent on these outside advisors. Often they will not charge fees overtly, but there are fees. They aren't providing you services out of the goodness of their hearts! There are **four drawbacks to depending on advisors**:

1. Their goals and your goals may diverge. Their ultimate goal is to make money for themselves or their firm.
2. They won't understand all of your needs.
3. They are focused on their area of expertise, whether it is financial products, real estate, banking products, life insurance products, etc. If your advisor works in a bank, they will

usually recommend banking products. If your advisor is a stock broker, they will tend to recommend stocks, bonds, and mutual funds, which they happen to sell. To a hammer, everything is a nail, so they say. So they will tend to recommend something for you that *they* are familiar with, rather than something that is the best for *you*.

4. In most cases, they do not take into account any desires for ethical investing. They will not be used to finding companies or funds that are not involved with alcohol, tobacco products, gun manufacturing, or whatever your ethical interest is. They will not, in most cases, have experience in finding companies that are proactive in environmental, social justice, pro-life, or other ethical concerns. You would have to do that yourself anyway, so you might as well do it from the start.

First, **follow the principle of diversification**. Have a proper mix of stocks and bonds. Diversify into as many industries as possible—not all one sector because it is flying high at that moment, or all utilities because they pay higher dividends.

Picking Your Own Stocks: Here is an approach that has worked well for me. First, I made a list of publicly traded companies that were **rated highly by their employees** as a good place to work. You can use Glass Door, a list from *Fortune*, or another source. My thinking is that when the workers enjoy working there, the company will do better in the long run. Since no one can know the short-term future, I am aiming at long-term results. That is your first "screen." Most of the companies that appear in the lists of best places to work are either nonprofits, or they are private companies without stock, so your list of stock companies after this screen will not be very long.

Then **screen out companies that do not pay a dividend**. My thinking here is that companies that pay dividends have established a track record of good earnings and have the confidence to pay their investors. It also helps to stabilize the price of the stock. It does not matter the size of the dividend—I include them if they pay anything at all. I also screen out companies that have a very high price-earnings ratio, say, above 50.

I broke this rule once. A local company went public and put out an IPO (initial public offering). Some friends told me that this was a great place to work, so I bought some of the stock on the day it was offered, even though IPOs never pay dividends. I more than doubled my money in only three years.

Then I apply my **ethical screen**. You have to decide this for yourself. You may not want to invest in companies that produce alcohol, or guns, or tobacco products, or pesticides for example. If you buy mutual funds, it is difficult to do this, but if you are doing it yourself, you can.

After these three screens, I am usually down to fewer than 20 companies. Then I **eliminate the duplicates in any one sector or industry**, until I am down to **seven or eight**, as recommended by King Solomon, and buy those stocks. Since this is a long-term investment, I usually don't look at them again until a year has gone by. I'm not anxious; I don't fret no matter what the market is doing. After a year, I look at the new version of Glass Door or other indices of good places to work, and see if any of the ones I bought has fallen off the list. Usually they don't—the list does not change radically from year to year. I check my progress. If fundamental things have changed, I may sell one or two, and replace them with others.

If there is a sudden downturn in the stock market, I **don't panic** and sell. Many people panicked in the Great Recession of 2008, and sold all their holdings at a loss after the stock market went down sharply. Then they missed the 60 percent rally that happened in the last nine months of 2009, so they lost twice.[8] Their investments are permanently diminished. If you have diversified, and picked worthy companies, you will have done everything you can do.

Final Task for Level 4: If you have done all these things for this level, you might want to consider **gifting some of your money to your heirs "with warm hands"**—i.e., while you are still alive. According to the IRS, you may give any individual up to $16,000 annually without triggering the federal gift tax.

At the same time, do not neglect to **help others around you to become resilient**, particularly those who are most vulnerable—the poor and homeless, new immigrants, single parents, families with special needs children, children in foster parent programs, and those who need adoption. Check out some ideas in Appendix 2 under Chapter 9.

Remember that this book is just to give you ideas and inspiration for where it is possible to go. Do your own research so that you will find out the best way for *you* to become financially resilient.

Savings from this step that can be invested: At this step, you will not even be paying mutual funds to invest your money, but instead you will pick your own investments and invest the money you would have paid to the funds in management fees.

---

8. https://www.nbcnews.com/id/wbna34635427

CHAPTER 10
HEALTH AND HYGIENE

Self-love, my liege, is not so vile a sin as self-neglect.
Shakespeare

People who cannot find time for recreation are obligated, sooner or later, to find time for illness.
John Wanamaker

To keep the body in good health is a duty...otherwise we shall not be able to keep our mind strong and clear.
Buddha

Be true to you teeth or your teeth will be false to you.
Dental proverb

If I had known I was going to live this long, I would have taken better care of myself.
Unknown

You are only as resilient as your health. Any big change in your environment or your situation, particularly a change for the worse, will cause stress, which impacts your health. If your health is already on the edge, the extra stress could cause some part of your body to fail just when you need more strength to be resilient. But if your general health is good, then the added stress of a temporary bad situation will not impact your heath very much in the short run.

There are just **four things** you must do to have basic bodily resilience: exercise, eat properly, get adequate sleep and relaxation, and take care of your teeth. Beyond those basics, strive to understand your own particular body, visit a physician regularly to get checked out, avoid addictions, and know the basics of first aid. Much of the investment here is in time to do those basic things and to gain knowledge, rather than a money investment.

1. Exercise: In order to get proper exercise, many people join health clubs or gyms, but these are a continuing drain on many budgets. If you buy a few pieces of equipment, you can do many of the same things at home. Trap: Many people buy the equipment, and then never use it. Solution: Use the things you intend to buy at your health club before you buy. There is also the buy-in impetus: You won't exercise, but if you buy a gym membership, it forces you to exercise so you don't feel like you wasted your money.

Solution: Exercise with a partner, or make an agreement with someone that you will each check up on the actual exercise of the other. At the very least, make a paper or virtual record of how much you actually exercised. The main thing is to do something about our modern tendency to have a sedentary lifestyle. If you consider walking and bicycling to be forms of transportation rather than as just recreation, as discussed in Chapter 7, you will automatically be getting a good amount of exercise.

Do not take performance enhancers as a shortcut instead of exercising and eating properly. In addition to being dangerous for your health, in any emergency situation the supply chains will break, and you will be left without your crutch and thus not resilient.

2. Eating properly can be summed up in the mantra of "everything in moderation." Some diets that totally eliminate whole classifications of foods such as carbs or fat are not healthy in the long run, so do your homework on them. If you are growing your own fruits and vegetables (Chapter 4), you will have a built-in incentive to eat healthy food. Improve your diet, step by step. Radical changes are often not good for you and are usually abandoned after a short time. But slow, steady changes will last.

3. Getting adequate sleep and relaxation is difficult in our modern hectic world. If you are in a condition of sleep deficit and an emergency comes up, your body will not be prepared for resilient action. Proper exercise and diet will help you to sleep—all these things are connected—so that if you are getting on the right track with one, it will help you with the others. But in addition, there are things you can do, eat, or drink that may help you to get adequate sleep.

If you stay up late, your body will signal you that you are low on energy, so you will snack to compensate. This results in weight gain. It seems paradoxical, but one of the best ways to lose weight is to be sure that you get enough sleep.[1]

If you are exercising, drinking, eating, and sleeping prop-

1. https://www.healthline.com/nutrition/sleep-and-weight-loss#TOC_TITLE_HDR_5

erly, in many cases **your weight** will take care of itself. If it does not, you may need to take more steps. Maintaining proper weight is very important for resilience—the prevalence of major illness or death due to COVID-19 increased in countries and among people who are overweight.[2] A person who is overweight is in danger of developing diabetes, heart disease, joint problems in the hips and knees, and many other unwelcome conditions.

Your body and mind need relaxation, so that you do not suffer from too much stress. To this end, **meditation** is recommended by many scientists. It helps to lower blood pressure and helps your body to regenerate. Do not meditate on nothing but on something or someone uplifting and worthwhile. To avoid focusing on a stressful or negative topic, it is more effective to refocus your thoughts on a calming or positive thing to replace it, rather than trying to empty your mind. After all, if someone says "Don't think about elephants"—where will your mind naturally go? Focus on penguins instead!

Another relaxation technique is known as autonomous sensory meridian response (**ASMR**). This is a calm, relaxing, stress-reducing reaction of your body to certain sounds, visual cues, or touch and personal attention from another person. They are gentle, comforting stimuli, often associated with nurturing activities such as having one's hair brushed. Some people experience these reactions from quiet, soothing music such as slow classical guitar or other stringed instruments. Others obtain this response by watching someone

2. https://www.rethinkobesity.com/obesity-covid-19.html?&utm_source=bing&utm_medium=cpc&utm_term=obesity%20coronavirus&utm_campaign=4_All_Shared_UB_COVID&utm_content=-dc_pcrid_73530123803395_pkw_obesity%20coronavirus_pmt_bp_slid__&msclkid=6fcb7af487d71691c49e1fce69a982dd&gclid=6fcb7af487d71691c49e1fce69a982dd&gclsrc=3p.ds

create a painting, sculpture, or other piece of art. Not everyone gets these responses, but for those who do, this can be a healthy way to relax and reduce stress. See Appendix 2 for an article that explains more about this phenomenon.

4. Taking care of your teeth is very important for overall health. Statistically, people who lose their teeth have shorter lifespans, and certainly do not enjoy their remaining years as much.[3] It is much easier and cheaper to protect your teeth from decay than to fix them after they have been damaged. Dental implants are very expensive!

There are many areas of knowledge that will help you with your health, just like with many of the other areas of resilience. Like with the area of skills (Chapter 8), the object is not to consider yourself an expert, but to know what things you can do, and to know when you need to call in someone with more training and professional experience.

As in all the other areas of resilience, if you are healthy you will be in a position to help others. First, you will physically be able to help them—you will have the strength and energy to do so. Secondly, you will be able to teach others by example and by words how they also can maintain their health.

Hygiene is a basic element of health, with its own levels and steps. To be resilient in hygiene is to be prepared with knowledge to do two things: use generic and fewer packaged products in order to save money and the environment, and be prepared to use alternative products or methods if your usual ones are not available due to a disaster.

---

3. https://healthnews.com/family-health/dental-and-oral-health/is-the-number-of-teeth-linked-to-our-life-expectancy/#:

HEALTH LEVEL 1: SIMPLE EXERCISES AND BASIC HEALTH STEPS

Simple Exercises: Make a commitment to yourself, your own health and your long-term resilience to get some vigorous exercise for at least a half an hour every day. Walk, run, bicycle, or swim. If you have an errand to do, make it a part of your walk. If you walk, do it at a brisk pace, or up a hill for part of the way so that your heart gets some exercise. This is more and more critical to your health as you get older. If you stop moving, you're dead!

If you jog or run, this has more benefits for your heart, but the pounding can be very hard on your joints. Therefore, be sure you invest in the proper running shoes so that your feet are cushioned. Swimming is actually the best all-round exercise, if you have access to a pool, but vigorous walking, jogging, or running is next best. Cycling is also very good, especially if you go up a moderate incline for part of the way. However you move, you want to give your heart some exercise by having it pump harder with some vigorous movement.

In addition to these moving exercises, do some simple strength exercises at home, such as push-ups and sit-ups, which can be done with no equipment at all. Combine this with stretching, such as the exercises given in Appendix 2. As a person gets older, exercises that involve balance are also important, so that you avert the general tendency to fall. Tai chi and other exercise regimes involve movements that are beneficial as we age.

If you have trouble motivating yourself to exercise, then do it with your spouse, a friend, or neighbor. Go to a local park for calisthenics. Many local parks have some exercise equipment—use it with a friend. Keep track of your progress. Some people do this with a Fitbit or other electronic device, but for others, a small notebook or a calendar is better.

Basic Health Steps: To **eat properly**, the first step is to make sure you are drinking enough water. Drink at least two liters (eight cups) of water every day. This would include all liquids, but be careful of consuming too much caffeine in tea and coffee. Also, sugared drinks should only be used on an occasional basis, and some of the sugar substitutes are questionable. Your total liquid intake will depend on your age, weight, sex, pregnancy and breastfeeding status, climate, and the amount of vigorous exercise you are doing. Most people do not drink enough. If you feel thirsty at any point in a day, it is an indication that your body is already in a state of partial dehydration, and has sent you a signal to that effect.

If you are not getting at least 7 ½ hours of **sleep** a night, then examine your usual schedule and habits. Avoid food, caffeine, and alcohol for several hours before bed, as well as stressful activity, such as watching an exciting film or TV show. But laughter is good, as well as relaxing music.

Visit a doctor regularly for a general checkup. Before this checkup, get a full blood test. Recently I did this, and discovered to my surprise that I was pre-diabetic, and had a deficiency of vitamin D. I solved the first problem with small modifications in my diet and the second with an inexpensive vitamin supplement. If I had not taken the blood test and had a general checkup, the pre-diabetic condition could have worsened to full-fledged diabetes, and I would have been taking pills or even injections for the rest of my life and made my body open to many other problems. The deficit of vitamin D could have led to bone loss, respiratory infections, and many other serious problems.

Visit a dentist regularly, at least once a year, to have your teeth cleaned and inspected. This way, small problems can be taken care of when they are small. At my last regular dentist visit, I was told that half of one molar had broken off. I had not felt anything amiss and had probably swallowed it with my food! The dentist put a crown on that tooth to prevent further danger to it. And it goes without saying that you should brush and floss every day.

If you think that any of these steps are time-consuming, consider that it will be even more inconvenient for you if you don't take them! Invest in your health! And as you do so, encourage those around you to do the same.

Acknowledge any **addictions** that you may have. Any addiction means that you have given control of part of your life to something else, and this is the opposite of resilience. The first step in treating an addiction is to admit to yourself that you are addicted. The second step is to seek accountability by admitting this to another person, such as at an AA or similar group meeting.

Savings from this step that can be invested: As in most steps of resilience, your savings will be the reduced costs of services you need. In this case, you will most likely pay less to doctors because you will be keeping yourself healthier. In my own case, I avoided the huge costs of becoming diabetic and vitamin deficient.

HEALTH LEVEL 2: SIMPLE EXERCISE EQUIPMENT, KNOW YOUR BODY, BASIC FIRST AID

Simple Exercise Equipment: For strength exercise, invest in some simple equipment you can use at home. Do not buy any expensive machines (Level 3) until you have established a routine of exercise. That way, you will not buy some expensive machine that just sits in your house taking up room, and you will have wasted your money. Simple things could include a pull-up bar you install in a doorway, some elastic exercise bands (also called "strength bands" or "resistance bands"), and perhaps some hand weights. Choose hand weights that will force to you exert yourself but allow you to do at least five to eight repetitions of an exercise. If you have to strain to do two or three, then they are too heavy.

Do not neglect your cardiovascular exercise—the kind of exercise that gets your heart pumping. If you are walking or running, then increase the distance, or add some hills. If the weather inhibits this in the winter (in a cold climate), or in the summer (in a hot climate), then you can use an exercise video in your own living room.

Know Your Body: Do your own research about your own medical conditions. If you continue to be overweight in spite of eating, sleeping, and exercising properly, this should be one of the first things you research. Healthcare knowledge is constantly changing. Research nutrition and possible herbal or nontraditional therapies that might relate to your situation. For example, if you have trouble sleeping, investigate essential oils or herbs that can help or ways to time or change your eating, exercise, and other activities to promote sleep. If you are subject to migraine headaches, research the various ways to treat them.

Basic First Aid: Someone, or better yet, several people in your household should have a basic knowledge of first aid. This includes how to clear a throat obstruction, how to treat simple cuts and burns, how to recognize and treat heat exhaustion or heat stroke (they are different!) if you live in a warm area, how to recognize and treat frostbite if you live in a cold area, how to take someone's temperature, how to handle a snakebite if you live where there are poisonous snakes, and what to do about possible food poisoning. Someone in your household should know CPR—cardiopulmonary resuscitation. Someone should also know what to do if your car was broken down in a remote area of your region with no cellphone service. This is a place for a household or small community to act together, where each person can focus on one particular aspect of first aid.

Be sure to have a basic first aid kit in your house, in your car, and with you when you go hiking or backpacking. This should include adhesive bandages (Band-Aids) in various sizes, antibiotic ointment, an emergency foil blanket, some pain tablets, and a small flashlight. The kit that is in your car should also have some water and food, such as granola bars, a book of matches, and a small knife.

Treating Addictions: The second step in dealing with an addiction is to get help from other people and from God. There are many programs dealing with specific addictions to alcohol, drugs, gambling, sex, etc. Twelve-step programs have a good track record in helping people to become free. Do not delay—join the appropriate group immediately.

Savings from this step that can be invested: In this step you may avoid visiting an urgent care clinic to treat something you can do yourself, and the huge costs of dealing with addiction.

HEALTH LEVEL 3: FULL EXERCISE EQUIPMENT, PREPARATION FOR EMERGENCIES, DEEPER KNOWLEDGE

Full Exercise Equipment: There are many machines you can buy now that do not take up half of a room in your house. If possible, you want to invest in a machine that can be used in a number of different ways to exercise all the major muscle groups on your arms, legs, and abdomen. If at all possible, try any machine before you buy it. Because many people buy a machine on a whim and then rarely use it, there are often used machines for sale—look on Craigslist, Facebook, or other online marketplaces or in your local newspaper, and you could save lot of money.

Again, do not forget to get your blood moving. You may also need some kind of machine that will allow you to get **cardio exercise** indoors. There are small, inexpensive "stair stepper" machines that will not take up much room. Or there are small devices that enable you to use your street bicycle indoors as a stationary exercise bicycle.

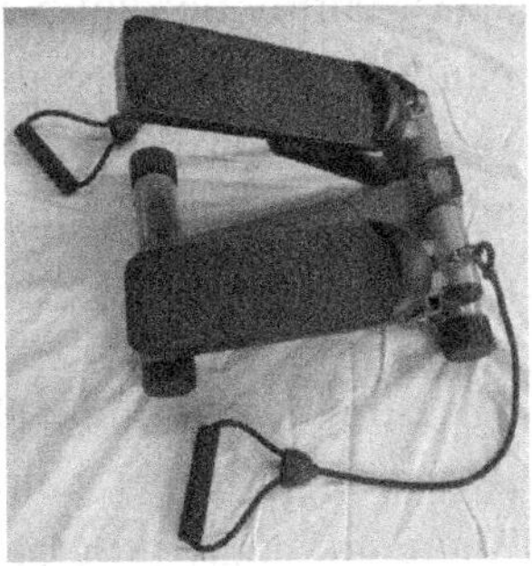

My stair-stepper

Emergency Preparedness: If there is someone in your household with specific medical needs, then resilience will require you to stock a supply of their specific items. If someone requires oxygen regularly, then try to obtain an oxygen concentrator rather than rely on delivered canisters.

Learn more advanced first aid. This includes how to splint a broken bone, and how to do some initial treatment of more severe cuts and burns. In both of these cases, you would normally take the person to an urgent care clinic or an emergency room of a hospital, but if these are far away or unavailable, you need to be resilient and prepared. When you learn how to use them, include more things in your first aid kit: butterfly closures, larger bandages with medical tape, and a clotting sponge.

Resilience does not mean total independence, or complete disconnection from larger society. In the context of emergency health care, it means that when bad things happen, you are able to do the best possible with what is available to you until more advanced assistance can be obtained. For a layperson, studying on your own and having the skills to deliver a baby in an emergency is excellent, but calling yourself a midwife and delivering babies without having more training is dangerous. Prudent resilience means being able to judge the difference between a problem you can begin to handle on your own, and when that problem would require more professional help.

Deeper Knowledge: Start educating yourself about the beneficial uses of various **herbs**, particularly the ones that you can grow yourself. These include lavender and chamomile as sleep aids, echinacea and elderberries to help immune function, dandelion root for liver health, aloe vera for skin treatment, ginger for nausea, mint for stomach ache, and many others. The proper use of herbs can lead to better health without resorting to harsh pharmaceuticals, which often have negative side effects. In addition, the supply chain for pharmaceuticals is often long and involves ingredients from overseas, which can create problems and decrease your resilience when there are disruptions. As always, advise your physician what you plan on taking so that they can monitor for any interactions between your herbs or supplements and your prescribed medications. See Appendix 2 under Chapter Ten for sources.

Also, **pass on what you learn** to someone else in your household or close community. This will do two things—it will increase the resilience of the community as a whole, and as you pass on the information, it will solidify that knowledge in your own mind and life.

Savings from this step that can be invested: At this step you will save what you would have paid for a gym membership because you have the proper equipment at home. You may also save money by using herbs to keep yourself healthy rather than more expensive and potentially harmful pharmaceuticals.

HEALTH LEVEL 4: ADVANCED KNOWLEDGE ON HERBS, BENEFICIAL FOODS, FIRST AID

Herbs and spices can have beneficial effects other than just make your food taste good. Garlic has antibiotic qualities. Ginger is helpful for stomach queasiness and has other benefits. Cinnamon helps to lower blood sugar. Honey is an antibiotic, and many people believe that local honey can help to ease allergies. Cloves can ease a toothache. Green tea, mint, turmeric, cayenne pepper, and other common foods and spices are also claimed to have medicinal qualities. Look up these things and use them when you have a mild condition. Then, for maximum resilience, see if you can grow the herbs that you find that you use the most.

. . .

Beneficial Foods: Research beneficial foods in general and particular ones for you. Your body may feel better when you eat certain fruits or vegetables or perhaps when you eat them at a certain time of day. Certain fruits may keep your bowels working well. In addition, there may be particular foods that your body does not tolerate so well. Some people do better if they do not eat gluten, even if they do not have a celiac condition (gluten-sensitive enteropathy). Others do better if they avoid red meat or caffeine.

More Advanced First Aid: Take your basic knowledge of first aid up another notch. Learn about how to take care of yourself in the event that you have no access to drugs or doctors. A classic reference book is called *Where There Is No Doctor—a village health care handbook*, by David Werner. The original is in Spanish: *Donde No Hay Doctor*. As the title says, this is a reference for an emergency situation when a doctor is not available. Your first choice in an emergency is to call 911 and get the person to a doctor as quickly as possible, but you must be flexible and prepared (resilient) in case you cannot do that.

Savings from this step that can be invested: You will save even more money by keeping yourself healthy and knowing the details of your own particular body.

Hygiene

Cleaning products are heavily advertised, which should alert you to the fact that they are heavily marked up and overpriced. If you are able to use simple or generic products, you will save money compared with the brand name ones. You will also make yourself more resilient in case some products become unavailable due to a disaster or due to supply chain problems.

HYGIENE LEVEL 1: CLEANSING PRODUCTS, TOILET PAPER, BABY, FEMININE HYGIENE, AND ELDERLY PRODUCTS

Cleaning Products: Most soap on the market is essentially the same active ingredients with different scents. It is possible to obtain a basic unscented soap that can be used for everything from washing dishes to washing the dog. The benefits include fewer chemicals and less worry about whether you have enough of all the different soaps you have been conditioned to use, thus making you more resilient.

The Toilet: Toilet paper can be avoided if one uses a bidet. This is the standard method in the Middle East and also in France. The benefits include reduced waste, more resilience, and fewer clogged drains. A bidet can easily be added to a standard toilet.

Babies, Feminine Hygiene, and the Elderly: Babies create lots of dirty diapers. Disposable diapers are convenient, especially when traveling, but fill up landfills. If you are at least prepared with some cloth diapers and know how to use them, you will be resilient if the disposable ones were somehow not available. The same is true for feminine hygiene products. What would you do if your usual products were unavailable? Have a reusable product on hand, know how to use it, and practice using it so that you know what to expect when an emergency happens. Then you will not panic, and you can share your answer with others at that time so that they also will not panic.

The elderly often have special products for incontinence and other conditions. Figure out what you would do if your usual product were not available.

Savings from this step that can be invested: You will reap savings from each of these practices, depending on how much you spent on them before.

HYGIENE LEVEL 2: DISASTER WASHING AND TOILET, ANIMAL CARE

Being resilient means being ready for a disaster, and in the hygiene area, being ready to use alternate methods for washing clothes and disposing of bodily wastes. This is not so much a matter of collecting materials as collecting knowledge and information so that you will be resilient. When there is a disaster, what will you do if the municipal water system has quit working? Since you would not be using these alternatives normally, they are more of a "prepping" step than an investment.

1. How will you wash your hands, and your body? Have some sanitizing wipes available.

2. How will you wash your dishes? Your clothes?

3. How will you do a #1 and a #2 if there is no water supply for your toilet?

a. "If it's yellow, let it mellow. If it's brown, flush it down."

b. See Chapter 6 for alternative water sources for flushing.

c. Use a bucket with a plastic bag in it, if there is a place nearby to take that bag.

d. Long term: Dig a pit toilet in your yard. To prepare for this now, research the best place in your yard to do this and the best way to do it, print out the results, and put it in a place where you will be able to find it when there is an emergency. This is not legal in most places, particularly inside city limits, but if there is a regional emergency, you gotta go somewhere!

Animal Care: Cats need litter boxes if they are kept inside, which means disposing of the litter. Many types of kitty litter use a special type of clay so that it "clumps." This is expensive and bad for the environment, and in a disaster situation, it probably will not be available.[4] If you used just dirt from your yard, it would be cheaper, and you would be more resilient. Put it in a separate bin from other compost. Or, you can buy natural cat litter made from wheat straw, corn stalks, or pine trees that have been formed into absorbent pellets.

Dog and cat waste contain bacteria, so this separate bin must be handled differently from ordinary compost, which decays by aerobic decomposition. Instead, if you want to compost it, a lactobacillus is added to the waste and fermented anaerobically (without air), thus killing any microbes present. This is called Bokashi composting, a process invented and used in Japan and Korea—see the link

---

4. https://www.conserve-energy-future.com/is-cat-litter-bad-for-environment.php

in Appendix 2. Like other forms of anaerobic digestion, it creates a liquid fertilizer at the bottom of the pail that must be drained off to prevent drowning the lactobacilli. The results are slightly acidic, so when the process is finished, it must be added to soil and allowed to compost in the regular way for an additional amount of time, unless the plants you are feeding like acidic conditions.

If you do not want to go compost it yourself, but your community composts its green waste, then you can put the animal waste in that barrel. Check with them first. But if your community simply grinds up the green waste and makes mulch out of it, then animal waste should not go there but into the ordinary waste bin. Either way, you do not want to put clumping kitty litter into the green waste barrel.

Savings from this step that can be invested: You could save the money you otherwise would spend on kitty litter.

HYGIENE LEVEL 3: HYGIENE FROM SCRATCH

Hygiene from Scratch: Just like cooking from scratch can save money, and may be the only way to eat if you live far from the nearest store, hygiene can be cheaper if you use generic or raw products. Laundry can be done without a dryer—on an old-fashioned clothesline. It can even be done without an electric washing machine. There are "scratch" ways to take care of feminine hygiene, baby diapers, the needs of elderly and disabled people, and for cleaning your environment. Some of these alternatives may be suited for your situation.

. . .

Savings from this step that can be invested: All of these simpler ways of doing things take more time but save money in the long run, and could be the only way to do things during a disaster.

CHAPTER 11
SPIRITUAL AND EMOTIONAL RESILIENCE

You shall know the truth, and the truth shall make you free.
Jesus
John 8:32

One who acts on truth is happy in this world and beyond.
Buddha

Anxiety in a man's heart weighs him down,
but a good word makes him glad.
Solomon
Proverbs 12:25

An important aspect of resilience is having a **spiritual and emotional foundation** that will survive the shocks that will come your way at some point in your life. Spiritual and emotional shocks most often come from people that we know well—spouses, parents, children, other relatives, close friends and neighbors. At some time in your life, one or more of them will let you down, or even betray you cruelly. Your leaders may also do this—bosses at work, political leaders that you have followed, and even leaders of spiritual communities. They are all human beings, and we humans are prone to failure in many ways. Will you have the resilience to carry on in spite of what they might do?

In the fog of conflict or crisis, it is not those who are physically strong or financially well-off who survive—it is those who keep a level head, do not panic, and calmly carry on despite setbacks. A spiritual and emotional foundation is a key element to that ability.

Those who have endured conflict or adversity over a long period are susceptible to a condition known as learned helplessness. This is when a person believes that they are in a long-term situation that they have no control over, so they stop trying to change their circumstances even when conditions change so that they have the ability to do so.[1] Essentially, they give up trying. A resilient spiritual and emotional foundation prevents this condition from taking place, and if a person is already in it, the building of such a foundation can enable the person to be lifted out of it.

Building a spiritual and emotional foundation requires **strong principles of life that will give you purpose and meaning.** If you know the purpose for which you are living, your circumstances can take a big hit, but you will keep on going. You need strong, ancient wisdom that has stood the test of time to guide you in such times. Without this, an increasing number of people today die "deaths of despair"—deaths due to suicide, alcoholic liver diseases, and drug overdoses.[2]

In dire circumstances, some who lack strong principles of life simply give up and die without actually suffering a mortal wound or disease. It has happened to people who are

---

1. https://www.psychologytoday.com/us/basics/learned-helplessness
2. https://www.acsh.org/news/2022/02/08/deaths-despair-16106

shipwrecked or prisoners of war and has been linked to extreme dopamine depletion.[3] In some cases, when one elderly spouse dies, the other also dies within a few hours or days because they have lost their reason for living.[4] A resilient life is one for which the reason for living does not depend on another person but is an enduring feature of your spiritual environment.

A spiritual and emotional foundation will also **alleviate loneliness**. In 2020 the Surgeon General of the United States said that loneliness has been associated with heart disease, high blood pressure, stroke, dementia, depression, and anxiety.[5] An increasing number of people of all ages report being lonely, and this accelerated during the pandemic because of lockdowns and fear.[6] Some of the reasons for this are not a mystery. The average household size in the U.S. has shrunk from 5.5 in 1910 to 3.3 in 1960 to about 2.5 in 2020, while the average physical house size has increased tremendously. In the past, most social interaction was face-to-face, but now it is increasingly in text messages and on social media, which often allows for little facial and bodily context.

What is the nature of a resilient spiritual foundation? First of all, it must be **based on reality**—on historical facts and logical principles. It cannot be based on a science fiction story, unsubstantiated legends, or one person's incoherent ramblings. When push comes to shove, a life based on these things will turn out to be built on shifting sand and will not

---

3. https://theconversation.com/give-up-itis-when-people-just-give-up-and-die-103727

4. A few examples from a Reddit thread: https://www.reddit.com/r/todayilearned/comments/oc11g6/til_of_psychogenic_death_when_a_person_gives_up/?rdt=58393

5. https://www.aarp.org/health/healthy-living/info-2020/vivek-murthy-loneliness.html#:

6. https://www.apa.org/news/press/releases/2022/05/covid-19-increase-loneliness

be resilient. A spiritual foundation based on historical facts and logical principles will make you able to withstand the storms of life.

Your spiritual foundation must likewise be **realistic about the nature of life**—what human beings and the universe are truly like. As the bumper sticker says, "Sh*t Happens." This includes not only natural disasters and accidents, which could be blamed on fate, but also evil things purposely done by other humans like murder, robbery, and vandalism, and on a bigger scale, war and institutional oppression. If an approach to life says that evil does not exist, it is not realistic. Likewise, if a philosophy claims that human beings are perfect-able in this life, you only have to look at a short history of war and conflict to realize this is not so. Similarly, if someone says that if you only follow their teaching, you are certain to become healthy and rich, walk away—it is manifestly not true and will eventually leave you disappointed or worse. Usually, people who teach this want you to donate to their ministry, thus making *them* rich and keeping *you* poor. Many such people maintain expensive programs on television and other media and need your donations to keep them going.

Your foundation also must **not blame some other group of people** for all that is wrong with the world today. Instead, it should **encourage your participation in finding solutions**. It will focus you on what you have the ability to mold or change, and not on what you can't. It must help you avoid self-pity, anxiety, and despair, which are the hidden enemies of resilience. Likewise, it should not blame even your own sexual, racial, ethnic, or religious group for all the evil around us. Honest self-examination is healthy, but despising yourself or any group to which you belong is not a way forward.

Your emotional and spiritual foundation must encourage

you and others to **develop good qualities**: love, joy, peace, patience, kindness, goodness, faithfulness, gentleness, self-control, and other good character traits. This is not putting on rose-colored glasses, through which some people do not see reality. Instead, it is accepting the world as it truly is but choosing to react to it in a positive way. Your foundation will help you ask and answer the question: Is what I'm doing helping or harming me and my community?

Your foundation must also provide an avenue for **forgiveness**—both for yourself and for others. If you harbor unforgiveness, it often leads to emotional and physical illness that keep you from being resilient.[7] A good spiritual foundation lets you see your anger and resentment from a genuine hurt from another person in a larger context—from God's point of view. This may allow you to let go of your resentment and anger and continue on with life.

Similarly, your foundation must equip you to **face suffering**—in your own life and also in others around you. Every resilient culture, religion, and philosophy gives its adherents an explanation for suffering so that it does not shipwreck them when it happens.

Emotional resilience also includes the attitude that does not take yourself and the world too seriously all the time. There must be **time for humor and laughter**. Animal and baby videos do it for me—and for many others as well, judging by their popularity. Many people enjoy cat videos in particular, which is a huge category on YouTube. Enjoy life with your human and animal companions.

In short, your foundation must be able to explain the existence of evil in the world and give you a path to avoid it

---

7. https://www.mayoclinic.org/healthy-lifestyle/adult-health/in-depth/forgiveness/art-20047692

as much as possible in your own life and in society in general.

Why are **some cultures around the world more resilient** than others? Some cultures existed for a time and then disappeared. Others have been around for millennia. The ones that have disappeared have often been "on top" for a while and have rested on their laurels. They assumed that they would always be on top and that whatever conditions allowed them to be there would continue. The Roman Empire might be an example—they assumed that their famous legions would always protect them and that the barbarians would always be weak, undisciplined rabble. In contrast, the cultures that have been around for several millennia have always been in a precarious position. They live in a tough neighborhood, so to speak, and have had to struggle for their existence, thus becoming resilient.

If you have not invested in your own spiritual foundation, then someone else is going to fill that void and try to push their foundation on you, and you will suffer (or perhaps enjoy) the result. Most likely, you will suffer needlessly. So take steps to invest in your own emotional and spiritual foundation and the foundation of the people around you.

LEVEL 1: READ AND ASK QUESTIONS, HAVE A PARTNER IN THIS QUEST

Invest in serious, time-tested spiritual literature such as a Bible. Read and study it, and write down questions. Find a trusted friend who knows something about that spiritual tradition and ask them questions. If you don't get anywhere, ask another person. If several from that tradition cannot help you, then choose another book or tradition. Check out several different books and traditions—don't commit yourself to the first thing that you encounter.

. . .

Ask questions: Who am I? Where did I come from and why? Where am I going? How am I going to get there? What is truth? What is good? Create your own questions. Start a journal and record your journey to the answers.

It is very difficult to be spiritually or emotionally resilient when you are alone. Before a setback or calamity overtakes you, **find a partner**, or several people who can help you assess the spiritual ideas you encounter and weather the storms that are sure to come.

Savings from this step that can be invested: This quest for emotional and spiritual resilience will, in the long run, save you money you might spend on counseling because you will become more grounded and less needful of professional help.

LEVEL 2: JOIN A SPIRITUAL COMMUNITY

After you have done some reading and investigation, join a church or other spiritual community, and become fully involved. How can you find a good spiritual community? I believe that a true spiritual community will:

- Genuinely care for you unconditionally, but without enabling harmful behavior.
- Help you develop and use your talents and gifts.
- Be led by a plurality of leadership with accountability, not just one charismatic person. It is extremely easy and very common for a spiritual community led by only one person to become manipulative or even abusive.

- Always act graciously and with love, even if someone leaves the group.
- Not be too interested in your money, and will leave you with some time for yourself.

Talk with people who have been in that church or spiritual community for some length of time. Ask them if they have observed the five points above in that community. If at all possible, join one that is physically close to you so you will not have difficulty getting together with them often. A study done in 2020 found that there was a decline in the percentage of people who reported "excellent" mental health compared to 2019. This is no surprise for a year marked by the pandemic. But those who attended (most likely online) church weekly reported a 4 percent *increase* in excellent responses.[8] Involvement in a spiritual community increases your mental, emotional, and spiritual resilience.

Savings from this step that can be invested: The social support that you receive in a spiritual community may save you the need to pay for professional help in many areas, and it can reduce your need for doctors and pharmaceuticals because you will be healthier.

LEVEL 3: PRACTICE SPIRITUALITY

Establish for yourself and your family or significant others **weekly, monthly, and annual rituals and celebrations** that give order and meaning to your life and serve as anchors. You should not feel enslaved to them, but instead, they are

---

8. https://www.catholicnewsagency.com/news/46871/only-frequent-church-attendees-avoided-downward-mental-health-trend-in-2020#:

there to guide your steps. Jews and Christians call the weekly day of rest the Sabbath, and some Jewish and Christian groups established rules for what one could and could not do on that day. But Jesus said, "The Sabbath was made for man, and not man for the Sabbath" (Mark 2:27). Thus we were not made to be slaves of any ritual, but rituals are meant to help us organize our lives. They can be as serious as weekly religious services, or as light as a weekly comedy program you watch together with special people. A monthly church picnic, an annual family reunion at a special place, or a weekly walk to a certain park will help mark the time and seasons.

Everyone needs to take a **day off once a week**. It has been scientifically established that people will accomplish more on the other days if they take one day off out of seven.[9] This weekly day of rest was only officially abolished twice in recorded history. The first time was during the French Revolution, when a 10-day week was proclaimed. When Napoleon took over, he returned France to the seven-day week. In 1929 the Soviet Union tried a calendar of 72 weeks of five days each, eliminating Saturday and Sunday specifically to eliminate both the Jewish and Christian days of corporate worship. This too was not successful. A day off means no work-related activity, if at all possible, but some physical recreation should be included as well as mental and emotional recreation or relaxation. If you work at a desk all week, then working in a garden can be relaxing, and a way to rest. But if you are a farmer and taking care of plants all week, then it is likely that working in a garden would not be relaxing, but rather sitting and reading a book.

Initiate and regularly practice **spiritual disciplines**,

---

9. https://www.inc.com/rhett-power/a-day-of-rest-12-scientific-reasons-it-works.html

which will strengthen your purpose, stability, clarity of thought, and wisdom, and through these qualities, your resilience. These disciplines can include prayer, meditation, reading and study of spiritual literature, memorization of inspiring quotes or passages, contemplation, retreats, fasting, and writing a journal of your thoughts. These things are most often done alone but can also be done with a spiritual partner. There are many variations of each one of these disciplines:

Prayer: This is a dialog with God, an encounter, an intimate relationship. It is both speaking and listening. It does not matter what position your body is in—you can be standing, sitting, kneeling, prostrating, or a combination of several of them. But it can help some people if the position is slightly different from your position for other activities, i.e. a special position used by you only for this. A quiet place with few distractions also helps so that you may concentrate.

Meditation: Many studies have shown that those who practice meditation and related disciplines have lower blood pressure and other beneficial physical and emotional benefits.[10] Do not meditate on nothing but on something or someone uplifting and worthwhile. In the New Testament, it says, "Whatever is true, whatever is honorable, whatever is just, whatever is pure, whatever is lovely, whatever is commendable, if there is any excellence, if there is anything worthy of praise, think about these things" (Philippians 4:8).

---

10. https://www.healthline.com/nutrition/12-benefits-of-meditation

Reading Spiritual Literature: Do not stop the reading you started in Level 1. Continue your reading and go deeper and wider. Pursue topics that relate to your situation in life. Ask your partner or trusted friends for suggestions as to what to read. If you have found a particular book helpful, consult the bibliography of that book for possible other books to read. Peruse a spiritual magazine that you trust and see if they have book reviews.

Study Spiritual Literature: Take a passage of something you have read in the Bible or other spiritual literature and look at it in depth. What does the passage tell you about the divine? What does it tell you about society and about yourself? Does it suggest any direction for you to follow? Write your thoughts and observations in a journal. Consult other authorities about the passage, but it is best to study it yourself first. This has two advantages. First, if you come to a conclusion which is later confirmed by others, it will have a stronger and more lasting effect on you. Second, if the first authority you consult leads you in one direction, it will bias how you look at the passage.

Memorization: As you read and study, you will find a sentence or passage here and there that expresses a key thought or concept very well. Memorize it! When you do, that concept will be with you wherever you go, even when the book where you saw it is not nearby. And when you teach the concept to someone else, you will be able to illustrate it with that quotation, thus giving your teaching the same authority that the original book has.

. . .

Contemplation: This involves thinking deeply about significant experiences, ideas, things, and people in your life so as to draw the maximum benefit from them. There are many things we encounter that we may skip lightly over, but a few deserve concentrated contemplation.

Retreats: Go somewhere out of your home for a half day, a whole day, or perhaps even several days. Take only a minimum amount of things with you, and if you take your phone, turn off the ringer and resolve not to use it during your retreat except for an emergency. Take a notebook and pen (or a computer or tablet) to write down the thoughts that will come to you. Take your spiritual literature and spend some of the time reading it. Spend time in quiet contemplation without the internet to distract you. There are locations around the country that provide a place for such retreats. If there is not one near you, then a campground or a quiet motel will also do.

Fasting: The main purpose of fasting is not the physical discipline, but the freeing of your time for concentrated prayer, meditation, contemplation, and other spiritual practices. Most people drink water during a fast, but you could also go on a "juice fast" of only drinking tea and juice, or a cold food fast of just trail mix or similar foods and water. Start with only a morning or an afternoon, and make subsequent fasts longer as you are ready for it.

Journal Writing: This can be simply writing briefly what happened during a day, a week, or a month, or it can include your thoughts about people or events. In the former case, it can help you simply recall the events of your life, so that at the end of a period of time you will know what you accomplished. In the latter case, it can be a form of contemplation, but one in which you preserve the results in writing.

Savings from this step that can be invested: It is hard to put a dollar value on these steps, but they can help your quality of life immensely.

LEVEL 4: TEACH OTHERS

When you have been a member of a spiritual community for a time, then use your gifts and talents to serve that community by teaching. Teach the younger members (in age or in experience) how to be spiritually and emotionally resilient, as you have become. You can start by teaching on an ad hoc basis or as a substitute for a regular teacher. As you feel comfortable sharing and teaching, then you can move up to regular teaching.

CHAPTER 12
INVEST IN YOUR NETWORK

Two are better than one, because they
have a good reward for their toil. For
if they fall, one will lift up his fellow.
Ecclesiastes 4:9-10

He alone loves the Creator perfectly,
who manifestsa pure love for his neighbor.
The Venerable Bede

If we fail to look after others when they need help,
who will look after us?
Buddha

Whoever brings blessing will be enriched,
and one who waters will himself be watered.
Proverbs 11:25

Let each of you look not only to his own interests,
but also to the interests of others.
Philippians 2:4

You are not an island. It does not help to say, "Your end of the boat is sinking." Therefore, even looking at things from a selfish perspective, when you help others around you to become more resilient, you also become more resilient. Look to family, friends, church, clubs, neighbors, and others to create networks of people who will help each other when there is a need. Networking means establishing and nurturing long-term, mutually beneficial relationships with a group of people. Even "preppers," who in the popular imagination prepare to hole up in a mountain hideout with only their family, say that one of the most important ways to prepare for disaster is to be a part of a group.[1]

An important aspect of resilience is having people around you who will support you, particularly when you are in a difficult situation. As Bill Withers sang, "**We all need somebody to lean on**." It may be an illness or death of a loved one, a financial shock, or a great disappointment, but something will happen in your life where you will need some kind of help. It could be just a shoulder to cry on or someone to sit nearby and commiserate with you. But it could be much more, depending on the situation.

These kinds of **networks illustrate the concept of inter-independence** on a human level. As an article in our local alternative newspaper put it, this is "solidarity, not charity."[2] The subtitle of the article says, "Mutual aid became more popular during the pandemic, and local organizers say it's here to stay." This mutual aid on a local, personal level builds inter-independence and resilience.

Alone, you will have a weak link. As the saying goes, a

---

1. https://www.consumerenergycenter.org/community-building-and-networking-among-preppers/
2. "Neighbors helping neighbors: During the pandemic, mutual aid groups proliferated throughout SLO County to help community members who fell through the cracks," *New Times*, July 1, 2021.

chain is only as strong as its weakest link. If your weakest area among the 11 previous chapters is providing for your water needs, then when a disaster comes, water will be where your life is fragile and not resilient. But if you are networked with a group, then it is likely that someone else in the group will be more prepared in that area, even if the group does not specifically plan for this. If the group does some planning, then all the links in the chain can definitely be covered by someone.

Networking also automatically alleviates one of the most prevalent ills of our modern life: loneliness. When you network with people over a common task, **loneliness goes away**. This was discussed in the previous chapter.

A study in 1979 found that the **risk of death is reduced** by half for those with the highest number of social ties compared to people with the fewest number of ties.[3] Studies since that time have identified some of the reasons for this. Social ties reduce stress, moderate inflammation and blood pressure, boost the release of healing hormones such as oxytocin, and can even ameliorate pain. If you have the right friends, they can help you avoid dangerous or harmful activities and encourage beneficial ones. People who commit mass murder are often described as loners, whereas those who are well-adjusted are those who have solid connections with others.

A study by researchers from Wellesley College, Notre Dame, and Ohio State University and circulated by the National Bureau of Economic Research in 2023 concluded that participation in religious services **reduced the incidence of "deaths of despair."**[4] This was actually noted in 2020 in a study conducted by the Chan School of Public

---

3. https://www.ncbi.nlm.nih.gov/pmc/articles/PMC3150158/
4. https://www.nber.org/system/files/working_papers/w30840/w30840.pdf

Health at Harvard University.[5] These are deaths due to suicide, or alcohol or drug abuse. Interestingly, it was not belief in anything in particular that made a significant difference in this study, nor personal practices such as prayer, but simply attendance at formal religious events. This indicates that the connections with other people that are made at such events are important for resilience, and why this fact is included in this chapter rather than the previous one.

LEVEL 1: JOIN A GROUP

Invest in strong bonds with a particular group of people around you—a spiritual community, a service club, a charitable organization, or even a group of close friends. Many areas have a "neighborhood watch" group. Establish bonds such that you will be able to say to yourself with confidence: **"If anything happens to me, they will have my back."** Of course, you also must be prepared to have their backs. And in order to protect the backs of others, you also must be as strong and resilient as possible yourself.

Mostly, this investment means time, but it also includes giving financially or physically (with donated food, clothing, toys, etc.) to local groups that help people in your community: churches, food banks, homeless shelters, shelters for abused or trafficked people, etc.

Savings from this step that can be invested: If the group that you join has an emergency supply of some item like a tool, then it is possible that you may not need to buy and

5. https://news.harvard.edu/gazette/story/2020/05/religious-services-may-lower-risk-of-deaths-of-despair/

stock the same item in your own stash. As for having your back, this is beyond price.

LEVEL 2: NETWORK

Join or establish a network to barter garden produce, share large tools or equipment, and trade services. Establish a community garden – maybe for your condo or HOA. Start a farmers market. Start a Freecycle Network affiliate in your area – it's a grassroots and entirely nonprofit movement of people who are giving (and getting) stuff for free in their own towns and neighborhoods, for the purpose of reuse and keeping good stuff out of landfills.[6]

Join or start a group of "gleaners"—people who go into fields of fruit or vegetables (with the permission of the owners) and pick up good food that was missed by the harvesters, and give this food to homeless shelters or food banks. Other gleaning groups focus on backyard fruit, and still others glean nearly expired food from grocery stores and restaurants.

Join a group that picks up trash on vacant lots, beaches, parks, or other public places. Many localities have groups that maintain hiking trails in local parks and open spaces.

In this group, share ideas about how the members can help one another with things beyond just the one subject or purpose of the group. For example, if you have a garden club, then share ideas about water, transportation, and other basic needs. If you are a member of a church, then share ideas about these needs as well.

Savings from this step that can be invested: The savings

6. https://www.freecycle.org/

here can be substantial if your group is organized. You will not need to keep so many specialized tools and other garden implements.

LEVEL 3: TEACH OTHERS

Teach what you know about resilience to others in your community. **Start with just one person.** Encourage him or her to go on and teach others, and you do the same. If you discover that you have a gift of teaching, try teaching a group. How will you know if you have a gift for it? First, you will enjoy doing it. It will feel natural to you, maybe not immediately, but after a short time. Second, people will tell you that you did it well. Third, the people you taught will tell you that they really benefited from what you taught. The ultimate way you will know is that those you taught will begin to teach others what you taught them. Your learning and teaching will be multiplied in the community.

Helping others is one of the ways that we create meaning in our lives, and teaching others is a major part of that. You can give a person material help, but it is more meaningful both for you and for the person you help if you can teach them something that will enable them to thrive long after you are not there.

If you find that teaching is really in your bones, and people tell you that they benefit from your teaching, then **record your teaching** and put it up on YouTube, Skillshare (they have nearly 2,000 classes!), Udemy.com (they claim 130,000 courses!), or another online platform. You will not only help others in their journey, but you might even earn money in the process. Udemy courses generally cost between $10 and $25 and include design, software, marketing, business, photography, music, health and fitness, finance and accounting, office productivity, arts and crafts, gaming, pet care, and travel. Of the topics covered in this book, they have courses in bread making, nutrition, gardening, woodworking, electric wiring, and permaculture, among others.

A more intensive way to teach is to take in **foster children.** There is a tremendous need for this everywhere. It is not something that everyone can do, but if you have a gift of working with children, it may be for you. If it is not your gifting, then perhaps in some way you can help a family you know that is doing it. Fostering children is very time-consuming, and those that do it may need help to do ordinary things like shopping or taking care of their yard.

Mentoring is needed for many things—all aspects of business, every profession, as well as just plain living. Those who are getting out of prison need a mentor to help them adjust to life on the outside, which is probably very different from when they went in, even if it was only for a few years. Whatever skill you have or area of expertise, your local university or community college would probably welcome your participation in mentoring students.

Savings from this step that can be invested: Some earn quite a bit of money by teaching skills and knowledge.

CHAPTER 13
FINAL WORD

Good luck is when opportunity meets preparation,
while bad luck is when lack of preparation meets reality.
Eliyahu Goldratt

Do what you can, with what you have, where you are.
Theodore Roosevelt

You are born looking like your parents.
You die looking like your decisions.
Anthony Zuniga

When you are resilient, you help your family, your community, your nation, and even the world as a whole become more resilient. When there is a downturn in the economy or a disaster, you will need less help from others and instead will be in a position to help others.

DIFFICULTIES WILL HAPPEN

I used the word "when" about a coming downturn or disaster because it is a certainty that these will happen. **Financial disasters** in the last few decades have included the dot-com bust in 2000, the terrorist attack of 9/11 that affected the economy, the 2008 Great Recession, and then the Pandemic Recession of 2020-21. Every region of the world is subject to at least one type of **natural disaster** and often several: hurricanes, tornadoes, earthquakes, tsunamis, large forest fires, widespread floods, or volcanic eruptions. Many of these natural disasters cause widespread outages of electricity, natural gas, water, and communications. **Political disruptions** even affect us in North America - we must now think about social unrest, insurrections, or worse. In all these cases, the resilient family or group of people will not only be able to take care of themselves but help others around them.

GET STARTED

The ideas presented here are just to get you started. **Pick one chapter** and go for something presented on Level 1 that fits your situation. If you live in an **urban apartment**, choose a solar small device charger from Chapter 1, a pot garden from Chapter 4 if you have a balcony or a sunny window, begin your emergency fund from Chapter 9, check out a spiritual book from Chapter 11, or attend a meeting from Chapter 12. If you live in a **small town**, you could check out some solar ovens from Chapter 2, look for a plant to forage from Chapter 4, a practical type of bicycle from Chapter 7, or a new hobby or skill from Chapter 8. If you live in a **rural area**, invest in an indoor/outdoor thermometer (Chapter 3), plant a raised-bed garden from Chapter 4, dehydrate some vegetables and fruit from your garden (Chapter 5), route the drain from your washing machine to water your trees (Chapter 6), take stock of your financial position from Chapter 9, or learn about essential oils from the internet (Chapter 10).

In some cases, you may have to **skip a level** because of where you live. If you live more than 10 miles from the nearest supermarket, then using a bicycle to get there may not be practical (Transportation - Chapter 7). If you live in an apartment or condo, then some of the techniques for harvesting rainwater may not work for you.

Challenge yourself! You will not feel fulfilled in life if you have not faced a challenge and prevailed.

BECOME INTER-INDEPENDENT

If a person achieves one of the upper levels in all of these areas of life, then that person is no longer dependent upon the global network. But, as we have seen, particularly in the later chapters, no one is totally independent either. Usually, we think of a person being either independent or inter-dependent. But there is a third way—we become **inter-independent**.

What would inter-independence look like? We could take an analogy from Chapter 1: Electricity. At Level Four, a person would be net zero in energy but still connected to the grid. The household would be producing as much as they are consuming, but at different times of the day and year, they would be drawing from or contributing from that grid.

In the other areas as well, the inter-independent household would be contributing to the overall community as well as drawing from it. We can give excess apples from our tree while receiving excess tomatoes from our neighbor's vines.

A person can be learning one skill while teaching another. Could we exist without our neighbor's tomatoes, or learning what our neighbor can teach? Yes, but our lives and the lives of our neighbors will be richer and fuller if we get together and share.

APPENDIX 1: COOKING FROM SCRATCH LEVEL 1

HEALTHY, CHEAPER GRANOLA

3 cups rolled oats

1 ½ cups of raw nuts/seeds: sliced almonds, small "baking" hazelnuts, pumpkin seeds, sunflower seeds, etc.

Optional spices: cinnamon, nutmeg, cardamom

1/3 cup vegetable oil

Put the oats, nuts, and spices in a 9 x 12 inch baking dish. Add the oil and mix, then smooth it out to an even layer. Bake for 12 minutes in a 350 F oven. Remove and allow to cool undisturbed before putting it in a container.

VINAIGRETTE SALAD DRESSING

2 ½ ounces vinegar (Ordinary dressing: white or apple cider vinegar. For premium, use wine vinegar.)

2 ½ Tbsp. water

5 ounces oil (Ordinary dressing: canola oil. For premium, use olive oil.)

½ tsp. dry onion flakes. ¼ tsp. cumin, oregano, thyme, dill, sage, black pepper. 1/8 tsp. garlic powder

2 tsp. tahini (optional, to make it thicker)

¼ tsp. turmeric powder (optional, to make it yellow and give an anti-inflammatory effect)

If you have a cruet, the levels for vinegar, water, and oil are marked for you. If not, just use the proportions given above in any handy container with a tight fitting lid. Add the vinegar, water, and spices to the container. Shake well. Add the tahini and shake again. Add the oil and shake a third time. No salt or sugar, unlike most store-bought dressings, and very tasty!

SPAGHETTI SAUCE

1 can tomato sauce

1 Tbsp. oil

oregano, basil, garlic, bay leaf, and fennel to taste. (Fennel will give it an Italian sausage taste.)

½ cup finely chopped yellow onion

optional extras: mushrooms, diced zucchini, small cubes of firm tofu, ground meat (beef, turkey, or pork)

Brown the onions and tofu or meat in the oil in a saucepan. Add the mushrooms and zucchini and saute for another minute. Add the tomato sauce and spices and simmer for about 10 minutes, and you are done! This will have half of the salt and sugar as canned spaghetti sauce, and cost significantly less.

CHICKEN SOUP

3 cups diced chicken
1 cup diced onion
½ tsp. poultry seasoning
1 Tbsp. vegetable oil
1 cup dry pasta, any shape
¼ tsp. black pepper
1 cup diced carrots
½ cup diced celery
1 cup any other vegetables you have around – cabbage, broccoli, cauliflower, green beans, etc.
6 cups water

Brown the onions and chicken in the oil. If the chicken is already cooked, add it with all the other ingredients and bring to a boil. Reduce to a simmer and cook for about 40 minutes.

BASIC WHOLE WHEAT BREAD FOR A BREAD MACHINE

2 ½ cups whole wheat flour
2 Tbsp. powdered milk
1 Tbsp. vegetable oil
1 ½ tsp. dry yeast
1 cup warm water

Variations: Add one small or 1/2 large apple, cored and cut into pieces, and decrease the water a bit.

Substitute rye, almond, acorn, or any other flour for one cup of the whole wheat.

Add spices, such as rosemary, cardamom, cinnamon, or thyme.

Put ingredients into your bread machine, press the "medium" button, and wait 2 ¼ hours until it beeps. Take it out immediately to cool.

SAUERKRAUT & KIMCHEE

1 head of cabbage
1 Tbsp. salt
red pepper flakes to taste, if making kimchi
a large jar and a round potato masher

Shred the cabbage. Mix with the salt, and with red pepper flakes (if making kimchi), and put it in the jar. Mash it down with the potato masher until the liquid covers the cabbage. Close the lid, and put it on your kitchen counter. Press the cabbage down once a day. After about four days, it will be ready! You can start eating it and put the remainder in the refrigerator.

APPENDIX 2: RESOURCES

CHAPTER 1: ELECTRICAL ENERGY

- **Solar panel reviews**: https://www.consumeraffairs.com/solar-energy/best-solar-panels.html
- **Wind turbine reviews**: https://ecavo.com/best-home-wind-turbines/
- https://www.youtube.com/watch?v=246iRwbyO9s
- **Horizontal vs vertical axis wind turbines**: https://www.youtube.com/watch?v=EM-gCvhQhPU
- **Tubercles (small bumps on the leading edge) increase efficiency**: https://www.youtube.com/watch?v=zWjA4qgFUJQ
- **Bladeless wind generator**: https://www.youtube.com/watch?v=pS2mhjdKdAA
- **Solid state electrostatic wind generator**: https://www.youtube.com/watch?v=l0UVryi0oEw

- **Prototype small hydroelectric generator**: https://www.youtube.com/watch?v=XjEgFlngZ04
- **Guide to small hydro**: https://www.micro-hydro-power.com/A-Guide-to-Hydro-Power.htm
- **Descriptions of nine hybrid hydro/solar/wind systems in BC, Canada**: http://www.homepower.ca/dc_hydro.htm
- **Slow-moving hydroelectric generator**: https://waterotor.com/
- **Hydrogen energy storage**: https://lavo.com.au/
- https://newatlas.com/energy/lavo-home-hydrogen-battery-storage/
- **AgroPhotoVoltaics**: https://www.youtube.com/watch?v=2ue53mBUtNY
- https://agsci.oregonstate.edu/newsroom/sustainable-farm-agrivoltaic
- • https://www.n-pr.org/2021/11/14/1054942590/solar-energy-colorado-garden-farm-land?

CHAPTER 2: COOKING AND HOT WATER

- Solar cookers review: https://solarpowernerd.com/best-solar-ovens/
- Box cooker instructions: https://solarcooking.fandom.com/wiki/Minimum_Solar_Box_Cooker
- Solar cookers for camping: https://www.rv.com/lifestyle-travel/cooking-grilling/everything-you-wanted-to-know-about-solar-cookers-for-camping/?utm_source=exacttarget&utm_medium=email&utm_campaign=RMN024735_05182022&scpc=

- Best portable rocket stoves 2020: https://www.youtube.com/watch?v=OhtVU-LjCcM
- DIY 8 rocket stove ideas: https://www.youtube.com/watch?v=FMhUFthG4bU
- Portable pressurized hot shower: https://www.nemoequipment.com/product/helio/
- Vehicle mounted hot shower: https://yakima.com/products/roadshower
- Home biogas generator (ready made): https://www.homebiogas.com/
- Make your own biogas generator: https://www.youtube.com/watch?v=T9P6ywewmmk (There are many such videos on YouTube)
- Biogas generators in developing countries: https://documents1.worldbank.org/curated/en/468451557843529960/pdf/The-Power-of-Dung-Lessons-Learned-from-On-Farm-Biodigester-Programs-in-Africa.pdf

CHAPTER 3: HEATING AND COOLING

- Passive House Institute U.S.: https://www.phius.org/home-page
- Passive houses in Massachusetts: Triple-Digit Heat, but No Electric Bill? For Passive Homeowners, 'It's Hard to Go Back' (msn.com)
- The Energy & Environmental Building Alliance: https://www.eeba.org/
- Retrofitting to Passive House Standards: https://www.youtube.com/watch?v=wN34zF7e4J8
- Retrofitting to NetZero in Alberta: https://www.youtube.com/watch?v=Qa_OWDPrxeI

- Heating without burning anything: https://www.youtube.com/watch?v=A8z2uPqYLAg
- Wood stoves: https://tinyhousehugeideas.com/most-efficient-wood-stoves/
- WikiHow – Cool yourself without air conditioning: https://www.wikihow.com/Cool-Yourself-Without-Air-Conditioning#:
- Cooling without air conditioning: https://www.bbc.com/future/article/20190822-are-there-alternatives-to-air-conditioning
- Natural heating and cooling: https://www.youtube.com/watch?v=SwiaaqKdtjw&t=1s
- Passive house in Texas: Texan builds stunning 'passive house' that uses 75% less electricity and literally makes him money: 'The best way to build' (msn.com)
- DIY solar air heater: https://www.youtube.com/watch?v=pHk0PX8pbWY
- https://www.youtube.com/watch?v=-phrKb5kFOM
- Comparison of two DIY heaters: https://www.youtube.com/watch?v=PyVPNOUpOVg

CHAPTER 4: FOOD

YouTube Channels

- Garden in the desert: *Growing in the Garden* (Phoenix area, Arizona)
- Garden a mild climate: *Self Sufficient Me* (Queensland, Australia)
- *Next Level Gardening* (southern California)
- Garden a cool climate: *The Gardening Channel with James Prigioni* (New Jersey)

- Garden a severe climate: *Jill Winger – the Homestead Mentor* (Wyoming)
- Garden a very severe climate: *Dong Jianyi* (Central Alberta)
- Urban gardening: *Epic Gardening* (San Diego)
- Grow a lot of food in a small garden (Alberta urban gardener) https://www.youtube.com/watch?v=KRBPgnYBsZs
- Planting from food scraps and many cooking topics: *Mary's Nest*
- How to make self-watering containers: https://www.youtube.com/watch?v=byBeDfKb02Q
- https://www.youtube.com/watch?v=dlxsapM_1ec
- Cold climate greenhouses: Simple Tek (channel) https://www.youtube.com/watch?v=pXPakvPzgpE
- https://www.youtube.com/watch?v=GofFoVDa-E0Walipini greenhouse: https://www.youtube.com/watch?v=Qvk7Sszh6fg
- General gardening: Melissa K. Norris – *Modern Homesteading* (Pacific Northwest)

Permaculture: *Verge Permaculture*

- Best Medicinal Herbs to Grow: https://www.youtube.com/watch?v=DZRIzGMr4jE
- Self-sufficient backyard: https://selfsufficient-backyard.com/
- Keeping deer out of your garden: https://www.youtube.com/watch?v=Ubbv-IY5Kkk
- Wicking container gardening: https://www.youtube.com/watch?v=G-0U5Jpq7Ik
- Ron Finley – *urban gangsta gardener*: https://www.youtube.com/watch?v=7GbGgr9ZnQQ

- Ted Talk: https://www.youtube.com/watch?v=EzZzZ_qpZ4w
- Beginning foraging: https://www.youtube.com/watch?v=ew5yeWqsWY8
- Benefits of stinging nettles: https://www.youtube.com/watch?v=lfn7py4owdY
- Collecting, processing & cooking acorns: https://www.youtube.com/watch?v=qLo3UWh-BN4
- General self-reliance, emphasis on food: https://practicalselfreliance.com/
- Emergency preparedness: • https://armed-forcesconnect.org/2022/05/18/how-to-layer-your-survival-kits-for-a-real-world-disaster/?

Books:

- *The Homesteading Handbook: A Back to Basics Guide to Growing Your Own Food, Canning, Keeping Chickens, Generating Your Own Energy, Crafting, Herbal Medicine, and More*. Abagail Gehring, Skyhorse Publishing, 2011.
- *The Mini Farming Bible: The Complete Guide to Self-Sufficiency on ¼ Acre*. Brett Markham, Skyhorse Publishing, 2014. Also, the *Mini Farming Handbook*.
- *40 Projects for Building Your Backyard Homestead: A Hands-on, Step-by-Step Sustainable-Living Guide*, David Toht, Creative Homeowner (publisher), 2013.
- *The Weekend Homesteader – A Twelve-Month Guide to Self-Sufficiency*, Anna Hess, Skyhorse Publishing, 2012.
- *Urban Homesteading – Heirloom Skills for*

Sustainable Living, Rachel Kaplan & K. Ruby Blume, Skyhorse Publishing, 2011.

- https://selfsufficient-backyard.com/

CHAPTER 5: COOKING AND PRESERVING

- Dehydrating: https://consumerreports.store/best-food-dehydrators/
- https://buyersguide.org/dehydrators/t/best?
- *The Food Dehydrating Bible – Grow It, Dry It, Enjoy It!*, Brett Markham, Skyhorse Publishing, 2014.
- Making a fruit or vegetable powder: https://www.youtube.com/watch?v=zDTiAHqlDx4
- Good basic canning book: *The All New Ball Book of Canning and Preserving: Over 350 of the best canned, jammed, pickled, and preserved recipes*, Ball Test Kitchen, TI Inc. Books, 2016.
- Pickling: Quick-pickle vegetables: https://www.youtube.com/watch?v=3PvMdbmf55Q
- No-sugar pickling: https://www.youtube.com/watch?v=cX_7xjTe4l8
- Processing Olives: https://honest-food.net/how-to-cure-green-olives/
- 25 Root cellar plans: https://morningchores.com/root-cellars/
- Trash can root cellar: https://www.treehugger.com/build-a-root-cellar-3016868

CHAPTER 6: WATER

- Earthships: www.earthshipglobal.com

- Earthship in tropical Florida: https://www.youtube.com/watch?v=ONzZORjb0PA
- Earthship project blueprint information: https://www.youtube.com/watch?v=8pWpKX2elI4
- Earthship article in the Washington Post: https://www.washingtonpost.com/climate-solutions/2022/01/04/earthship-houses-climate-change/?
- *Hacking the Earthship: In Search of an Earth-Shelter that WORKS for EveryBody*, Rachel Preston Prinz et al, Archinia Publishing, 2015
- Fog catchers in Peru: https://www.youtube.com/watch?v=G4GHGBov15U
- https://www.youtube.com/watch?v=YxRONAZoMDk
- Fog catchers in Morocco; Fog harps: https://www.youtube.com/watch?v=NBhFxXT9mUQ
- DIY fog catcher: https://www.youtube.com/watch?v=k7Vfp4aAuKE&t=270s
- Solar Hydro Panels: Renewable drinking water straight to your home tap | SOURCE Water
- Cities and businesses using condensation from air conditioners: https://www.bloomberg.com/news/articles/2021-05-11/dry-cities-look-to-reuse-air-conditioner-water
- Atmospheric water generators: https://www.watergen.com/
- Off-grid living, tiny houses, unusual living: Exploring Alternatives (YouTube channel)

CHAPTER 7: TRANSPORTATION

PEBL velomobile (pedal electric vehicle): https://www.better.bike/

ELF velomobile (pedal electric vehicle): https://organic transit.com/

Electric bike-cars review: https://electrek.co/2018/06/04/solar-powered-electric-bike-cars-elf-and-pebl-might-just-be-weird-enough-to-work/

European 4-wheel e-bike: https://www.youtube.com/watch?v=d5nV1vkSMp0

Top 9 electric sit-down scooters for sale in U.S.: https://www.youtube.com/watch?v=DCwcrh50NhA

GEM Neighborhood Electric Vehicle: https://gem.polaris.com/en-us/

Spanish microcar with removable batteries rechargable inside your house, solving the problem of living in an apartment: https://www.youtube.com/watch?v=q1LHh6FkpuI

Personal electric transportation: https://www.youtube.com/watch?v=dJa1Tic3V2Y

Off-road electric scooters: https://www.youtube.com/watch?v=EEyVmJrxTBQ

10 electric bikes under $2000: https://www.youtube.com/watch?v=Bi8WlPXK6Bw

Aptera electric car – 2-seater, solar panels, 1000 mile range: https://www.aptera.us/

Another California electric car startup: https://www.youtube.com/watch?v=k6JMoMQHvNA

Making bio diesel: https://www.youtube.com/watch?v=4QEWsWAsRK8&t=188s

CHAPTER 8: SKILLS

YouTube has many videos how to do things. Look them up by subject.

Video courses:

- www.Skillshare.com

- www.udemy.com

Possible places to market your skills:

- Facebook Marketplace
- Amazon
- Etsy.com
- Fiverr.com

CHAPTER 9: FINANCIAL

- Basic information on 529 College Savings Plans: https://www.sec.gov/reportspubs/investor-publications/investorpubsintro529htm.html
- Consortium of work colleges (tuition free): https://workcolleges.org/
- Williamson College of the Trades (3 year program, no cost for tuition, room & board):
- https://www.williamson.edu/about/
- Free resources for getting out of debt and generally sound financial advice: www.daveramsey.com.
- Write a will for free: https://www.lawdepot.com
- Write a will without a lawyer: https://info.legalzoom.com/article/how-make-will-without-lawyer
- Living will for medical treatment: https://www.formfindr.com
- Legal forms: www.nolo.com

Examples of organizations that help people to rise up and be resilient:

- Bottom level: The Salvation Army: https://www.salvationarmyusa.org/usn/
- Network of Community Loan Coops: https://seedcommons.org/about-seed-commons/
- Work training program for single mothers in Philadelphia: https://www.everygoodgift.org/shop/
- Helping the homeless get on their feet in Missouri: https://wateredgardens.org/
- Training homeless in woodworking in Indianapolis: https://pdindy.com/products/
- Organizations engaging in effective compassion: https://world.wng.org/categories/ministries

CHAPTER 10: HEALTH

- Inexpensive portable stair-stepper: https://www.walmart.com/ip/Stamina-Mini-Stepper-with-Monitor-Low-impact-black-and-gray-stepper-great-design-for-at-home-workouts/28132535
- Resistance Band workout for beginners: https://www.youtube.com/watch?v=Lk5PisETE9I
- Article: What is ASMR?: https://www.sleep.org/what-is-asmr/
- *Unwind Your Mind – the life-changing power of ASMR*, Emma WhispersRed, Harper One, 2019. "Harness the healing power of sound."
- Bokashi supplies: https://store.bokashicycle.com/Bokashi-Culture-Mix-Supplies_c_9.html

CHAPTER 11: EMOTIONAL AND SPIRITUAL RESILIENCE

- Religion improves your health: https://www.usatoday.com/story/opinion/2016/10/28/religion-church-attendance-mortality-column/92676964/
- *Spiritual Disciplines Handbook – Practices That Transform Us*, Adele Ahlberg Calhoun, IVP Books, 2015

Chapter 12: Network and Community

- Freecycle groups: https://www.freecycle.org/
- How to network: https://www.scienceofpeople.com/networking/